The Mobile Agent
Rendezvous Problem in the Ring

Synthesis Lectures on Distributed Computing Theory

Editor

Nancy Lynch, *Massachusetts Institute of Technology*

Synthesis Lectures on Distributed Computing Theory is edited by Nancy Lynch of the Massachusetts Institute of Technology. The series will publish 50- to 150 page publications on topics pertaining to distributed computing theory. The scope will largely follow the purview of premier information and computer science conferences, such as ACM PODC, DISC, SPAA, OPODIS, CONCUR, DialM-POMC, ICDCS, SODA, Sirocco, SSS, and related conferences. Potential topics include, but not are limited to: distributed algorithms and lower bounds, algorithm design methods, formal modeling and verification of distributed algorithms, and concurrent data structures.

The Mobile Agent Rendezvous Problem in the Ring
Evangelos Kranakis, Danny Krizanc, and Euripides Markou
2010

The Mobile Agent Rendezvous Problem in the Ring

Evangelos Kranakis, Danny Krizanc, and Euripides Markou

ISBN: 978-3-031-00871-9   paperback
ISBN: 978-3-031-01999-9   ebook

DOI 10.1007/978-3-031-01999-9

A Publication in the Springer series
SYNTHESIS LECTURES ON DISTRIBUTED COMPUTING THEORY

Lecture #1
Series Editor: Nancy Lynch, *Massachusetts Institute of Technology*
Series ISSN
Synthesis Lectures on Distributed Computing Theory
ISSN pending.

The Mobile Agent
Rendezvous Problem in the Ring

Evangelos Kranakis
Carleton University, Ontario, Canada

Danny Krizanc
Wesleyan University, Connecticut, USA

Euripides Markou
University of Central Greece, Fthiotida, Greece

SYNTHESIS LECTURES ON DISTRIBUTED COMPUTING THEORY #1

ABSTRACT

Mobile agent computing is being used in fields as diverse as artificial intelligence, computational economics and robotics. Agents' ability to adapt dynamically and execute asynchronously and autonomously brings potential advantages in terms of fault-tolerance, flexibility and simplicity.

This monograph focuses on studying mobile agents as modelled in distributed systems research and in particular within the framework of research performed in the distributed algorithms community. It studies the fundamental question of how to achieve *rendezvous*, the gathering of two or more agents at the same node of a network. Like leader election, such an operation is a useful subroutine in more general computations that may require the agents to synchronize, share information, divide up chores, etc.

The work provides an introduction to the algorithmic issues raised by the rendezvous problem in the distributed computing setting. For the most part our investigation concentrates on the simplest case of two agents attempting to rendezvous on a ring network. Other situations including multiple agents, faulty nodes and other topologies are also examined. An extensive bibliography provides many pointers to related work not covered in the text.

The presentation has a distinctly algorithmic, rigorous, distributed computing flavor and most results should be easily accessible to advanced undergraduate and graduate students in computer science and mathematics departments.

KEYWORDS

mobile agent, network, rendezvous, ring, token, torus, tree, time-memory trade offs, black hole

... to Eda, Maura, and Elsa

We hear within us the perpetual call: There is the problem. Seek its solution. You can find it by pure reason, for in mathematics there is no *ignorabimus*.

David Hilbert, 1903 (60)[page 445]

Contents

Preface

The paradigm of mobile agent computing has seen use in fields as diverse as artificial intelligence, computational economics and robotics. Agents bring potential advantages in terms of efficiency, fault-tolerance, flexibility and simplicity.

In this monograph we are interested in studying mobile agents as modelled in distributed systems research and in particular within the framework of research performed in the distributed algorithms community. In this literature, the agents are generally modelled as automata that move on a network modelled as a graph.

A fundamental question in this area is how to achieve *rendezvous*, the gathering of two or more agents at the same node of the network. Like leader election, such an operation is a useful subroutine in more general computations that may require the agents to synchronize, share information, divide up chores, etc.

The purpose of this book is to provide an introduction to the algorithmic issues raised by the rendezvous problem in the distributed computing setting. For the most part our investigation concentrates on the simplest case of two agents attempting to rendezvous on a ring network. Other situations including multiple agents, faulty nodes and other topologies are also examined. An extensive bibliography provides many pointers to related work not covered in the text.

The presentation has a distinctly algorithmic, rigorous, distributed computing flavor and most results should be easily accessible to advanced undergraduate and graduate students in computer science and mathematics departments. The reader will no doubt notice that several (albeit not all) theorems are based on fairly simple algorithms and the eager student is strongly encouraged to attempt the proofs on his/her own before looking at them.

We are indebted to the many friends, colleagues and research collaborators for learning from the numerous enjoyable discussions the topics presented in this book. These include Jurek Czyzowicz, Krzysztof Diks, Stefan Dobrev, Paola Flocchini, Pierre Fraigniaud, Leszek Gasieniec, Nicola Hanusse, Dimitris Kavvadias, Lefteris M. Kirousis, Ralf Klasing, Flaminia Luccio, Patrick Morin, Andrzej Pelc, Paolo Penna, Giuseppe Prencipe, Sergio Rajsbaum, Nicola Santoro, Cindy Sawchuk, Yiannis Stamatiou, Jorge Urrutia, and Peter Widmayer.

We would also like to thank Nancy Lynch for giving us the opportunity to publish this monograph, Diane Cerra for her support and encouragement as well as the support staff at Morgan and Claypool for their help in putting it all together.

March, 2010

Evangelos Kranakis
Ottawa, ON, Canada

Danny Krizanc
Middletown, CT, USA

Euripides Markou
Lamia, Greece

Research supported in part by NSERC (Natural Sciences and Engineering Research Council of Canada) and MITACS (Mathematics of Information Technology and Complex Systems) grants.

CHAPTER 1

Models for Mobile Agent Computing

1.1 INTRODUCTION

The concept of an agent working on behalf of another entity is a simple yet powerful abstraction that has been found useful in many areas of computing. In certain applications, adding the capability of movement to an agent can lead to further simplifications and efficiencies. Consider, for example, the following scenarios:

- *Network Maintenance.* In a heterogeneous network, it is necessary to regularly provide nodes with software updates, check for security vulnerabilities, etc. A simple approach to this would be to have an agent (or team of agents) regularly visit the nodes to determine what maintenance is required and to perform it.

- *Electronic Commerce.* In some situations, the success of a given transaction requires the near simultaneous success of multiple transactions. For example, when preparing for a trip, one may be purchasing airline tickets, making hotel reservations and scheduling meetings. A mobile agent can move between applications, making sure that all transactions are ready before committing to any.

- *Intelligent Search.* When searching for information across multiple sources, it is often the case that queries must be adapted depending on the answers received. An agent with the ability to filter information locally and adapt its behavior while moving between sources is potentially more efficient than one that always has to return to the user for guidance.

- *Robotic Exploration.* In a potentially dangerous environment, it makes sense for robots to be the first to explore a region. A simple and potentially cheap solution is to have a team of small communicating robots (agents) cooperatively explore rather than one expensive human-controlled robot.

In this monograph, we concentrate on modeling agents as developed in distributed systems research (see (79)), though much of what we discuss could be applied in other domains such as artificial intelligence (e.g., intelligent multiagent systems (95)), robotics (e.g., autonomous mobile robots (85)), computational economics (e.g., agent-based economic modelling (93)) and networking (e.g., active networks (92)). We first informally describe what we mean by a mobile agent system and discuss the potential advantages and disadvantages of such systems. We then develop a framework for an algorithmic theory of mobile agents. Finally, we survey how the theory has been applied to analyze the problem of achieving mobile agent rendezvous in a network with emphasis on the ring network.

1.1.1   WHAT IS A MOBILE AGENT?

Mobile agents are autonomous, goal-oriented software entities that can transport their state from one computational environment to the next and resume its execution in the new environment, thus remaining active as they migrate between computers. This makes them a powerful tool for implementing distributed applications in computer networks. To be more precise, we imagine a mobile agent to be a software entity endowed with the following properties:

- *Autonomy.* As is the case with real world agents such as travel agents, software agents should work with some degree of independence from their creator. They should be able to make at least some decisions without the need to consult a central authority.

- *Mobility.* In the case of mobile agents, we insist that they have the ability to move from node to node in a distributed system. When such an agent moves, it is assumed that it encapsulates some or all of its state to move with it.

Beyond the above, a number of researchers include the following attributes in their definition of a mobile agent:

- *Interactivity.* Obviously, an agent must be able to interact with its environment, to make queries of nodes it visits, to report its findings, etc. But in many (possibly most) applications, we imagine that more than one agent is present, and the agents themselves are able to interact. Again, in most instances, this is likely to be cooperative behavior, but competitive behavior is also possible. The exact form of this interaction depends upon the system but usually involves some sort of communication, either by means of message passing or shared memory.

- *Adaptability.* The usefulness of an agent increases significantly with its ability to adapt to new situations, to learn from previous experience and to model correctly the intentions of the user who created it as well as those of the agents it encounters.

It is our goal to develop a flexible framework in which systems exhibiting any subset of the above properties can be analyzed.

1.1.2   WHY MOBILE AGENTS?

The applications one has in mind for mobile agents can generally be solved by traditional distributed computing approaches so why use them? While not a panacea, it can be argued that they offer a number of advantages over the standard solutions including:

- *Efficiency.* Assuming that the agents are sufficiently compact (program plus state), they offer potential savings in both latency and network bandwidth. In a situation where n sites must be visited in sequential order, where for instance the output from one site is used as part of the input to the next, a mobile agent can perform the task by moving along an n edge cycle incurring the cost of n communication steps whereas the communication pattern of a centrally located agent would be a star with $2n$ communication steps (to and from each site) required. In a situation where parallel access to the sites is possible, then a team of mobile agents (in this case sometimes referred to as *clones*) can visit all of the sites faster than a single stationary agent.

- *Fault-tolerance.* In situations where a user has limited or even intermittent connectivity to the network (e.g., mobile devices), a mobile agent may overcome this deficit by acting on behalf of the user during blackout periods and returning useful information when connectivity returns. In situations where nodes may go down on a regular basis with limited notice, a mobile agent can potentially move to another node and continue operating.

- *Flexibility.* It is generally easy to add features to agents that allow them to adapt their behavior to new conditions. More sophisticated agents may be designed to incorporate learning from past experience.

- *Ease of Use.* In many situations, it is natural both from the perspective of the user and the programmer to imagine that they are dealing with autonomous agents. In some instances, this improves the user's experience of the application. In other instances, an agent-based paradigm makes the system's design and implementation easier to perform. While these benefits are hard to quantify, they can be as important as the above.

In order to evaluate (at least theoretically) the above claims, especially those concerning efficiency and fault-tolerance, a model for analyzing the behavior of mobile agent algorithms is needed.

1.2   AN ALGORITHMIC MODEL FOR MOBILE AGENTS

Work on the design and analysis of algorithms proceeds within the confines of a given algorithmic model. For example, a popular model in which sequential algorithms are analyzed is the standard RAM model of computing. For parallel algorithm analysis, a number of models, such as the PRAM, are used. For each paradigm, an appropriate algorithmic model is developed. In general, a model is an abstraction which attempts to capture the most important aspects of a computational process. It consists of a description of allowable operations (or transitions) that can be performed by the process. For example, the RAM model allows for read/write operations, arithmetic operations, etc. Once this is established, one generally defines a set of measurable resources of interest, e.g., time (number of primitive operations), space (number of registers or potential states), etc. At this point, one is ready to analyze algorithms for well-defined problems (often expressed as input-output conditions). Assuming the model captures the computation sufficiently accurately, it can be used to:

- analyze the complexity (the amount of a given resource used) of different algorithms for a problem in order to determine which is most efficient, and

- determine lower bounds on the complexity of any algorithm for a given problem or relate the complexities of different problems.

In order to model mobile agents, we must model both the agents themselves and the networks that host them. Rather than describe one model, we present a framework for a class of related models for both hosts and agents, among which one may choose a model to be used, depending upon the application one has mind.

1.2.1   MOBILE AGENTS

We are interested in modeling a set of software entities that act more or less autonomously from their originator and have the ability to move from node to node in a distributed network maintaining some sort of state with the nodes of the network providing some amount of (possibly longterm) storage and computational support. Either explicitly or implicitly, such a mobile (software) agent is most often modeled using a finite automaton consisting of a set of states and a transition function. The transition function takes as input the agent's current state as well as possibly the state of the node it resides in and outputs a new agent state, possible modifications to the current node's state and a possible move to another node. In some instances, we consider probabilistic automata, which have available a source of randomness that is used as part of their input. Such agents are referred to as *randomized* agents.

An important property to consider is whether or not the agents are distinguishable, i.e., if they have distinct labels or identities. Agents without identities are referred to as *anonymous* agents. Anonymous agents are limited to running precisely the same program, i.e., they are identical finite automata. As the identity is assumed to be part of the starting state of the automaton, agents with identities have the potential to run different programs.

The knowledge the agent has about the network it is on and about the other agents can make a difference in the solvability and efficiency of many problems. For example, knowledge of the size of the network or its topology or the number of and identities of the other agents may be used as part of the agent's program. If available to the agents, this information is assumed to be part of its starting state. (One could imagine situations where the information is made available by the nodes of the network and not necessarily encoded in the agent.)

An important consideration for the case of teams of agents is how they interact. For example, are agents able to detect the presence of other agents at a given node? Assuming that the agents are designed to interact, the method through which they communicate is an important aspect of any model. For example, one might consider a case where agents have the ability to read the state of other agents residing at the same node. Or one might only allow communication via a shared memory space or via message passing. Other properties that may be considered include whether or not the agents have the ability to "clone" themselves, i.e., produce new copies of themselves with the same functionality and whether or not they have the ability to "merge" upon meeting (sometimes referred to as "sticky" agents).

1.2.2   DISTRIBUTED NETWORKS

The model of a distributed network is essentially inherited directly from the algorithmic theory of distributed computing (see for example (75) or (86)). We model the network by a graph whose vertices comprise the computing nodes and edges correspond to communication links.

The nodes of the network may or may not have distinct identities. In an *anonymous* network, the nodes have no identities. In particular, this means that an agent can not distinguish two nodes except perhaps by their degree. The outgoing edges of a node are usually thought of as distinguishable, but an important distinction is made between a globally consistent edge-labeling versus a locally independent edge-labeling. A simple example is the case of a ring where clockwise and counter-clockwise edges are marked consistently around the ring in one case, and the edges are arbitrarily - say by an adversary - marked 1 and 2 in the other case. If the labeling satisfies certain coding properties, it is called a *sense of direction* (55). Sense of direction has turned out to greatly effect the solvability and efficiency of solution of a number of problems in distributed computing and has been shown to be important for the study of mobile agents as well.

Networks are also classified by how they deal with time. In a synchronous network, there exists a global clock available to all nodes. This global clock is inherited by the agents. In particular, it is usually assumed that in a single step an agent arrives at a node, performs some calculation, and exits the node and that all agents are performing these tasks "in sync." In an asynchronous network, such a global clock is not available. In this case, the speed with which an agent computes or moves between nodes, while guaranteed to be finite, is not a priori determined.

We have to consider the resources provided by the nodes to the agents. All nodes are assumed to provide enough space to store the agent temporarily and computing power for it to perform its tasks. (The case of malicious nodes refusing agents or even worse destroying agents - so-called *black holes* - is also sometimes considered.) It is also assumed that the nodes will transport the agents to other nodes upon request. Beyond these basic services, one considers nodes that might provide some form of long-term storage, i.e., state that is left behind when the agent leaves. This long-term storage may or may not be shared among all agents using the services of the node. So, for example, this memory might be best thought of as a *whiteboard* on which an agent can leave messages for themselves or for other agents. A further service the node may provide to the agents is mechanism for sending and/or receiving messages via message passing.

Finally, when analyzing fault-tolerance, one has to consider how a host network component might fail. Again, here we inherit the standard network fault models considered in distributed computing such as crash failures, omission failures, Byzantine failures, etc. One might also consider failures that do not effect the working of the network but only the agent subsystem, e.g., loss of shared data.

1.2.3   RESOURCE MEASURES

For a given choice of agent plus network model, there are a number of resources of interest for which one can define a complexity measure. Measures of paramount concern are that reflect the time and bandwidth efficiency of a given algorithm. In the synchronous setting, it is clear that to measure time one should use the assumed global clock. In an asynchronous setting the situation is not so clear though in most instances authors choose to evaluate what the worst case time would be assuming that time proceeded synchronously. The total bandwidth consumed by the agent depends upon its size as well as the number of moves it makes during an execution of its algorithm. Generally, the size of an agent is identified with the number of bits required to encode its states, i.e., it is proportional to the log base two of the number of possible states. If the agent sends messages, then the size and number of these messages must also count towards any measure of its bandwidth. Other complexity measurements of interest include the size of shared memory required at each node, assuming the agents communicate via shared memory, the number of random bits used by a randomized agent and the number and kind of faults an algorithm can successfully deal with.

1.3   MOBILE AGENT RENDEZVOUS

A natural problem to study for any multiagent mobile system is that of rendezvous. Requiring agents to meet in order to synchronize, share information, divide up duties, etc. is a fundamental operation, useful as a subroutine in more complicated applications such as web-crawling, peer-to-peer lookup, meeting scheduling, etc. Given a particular agent model and network model, a set of agents distributed arbitrarily over the nodes of the network are said to *rendezvous* if after running their programs after some finite time, they all occupy the same node of the network at the same time. As is often the case, researchers are interested in examining cases that expose the limits of the problem being studied. For rendezvous, perhaps, the simplest interesting case is that of two agents attempting to rendezvous on a ring network. Of special interest is the highly symmetric case of anonymous agents on an anonymous network. In particular, below, we consider the standard model for an anonymous synchronous oriented ring (11) where

1. the nodes have no identities, i.e., the agents can not distinguish between the nodes,

2. the computation proceeds in synchronous steps, and

3. the edges of each node are labeled left and right in a consistent fashion.

We model the agents as deterministic finite automata $A = <S, \delta, s_0>$ where S is the set of states of the automata including s_0 the initial state and the special state halt, and $\delta : S \times P \rightarrow S \times M$ where $P = \{present, notpresent\}$ represents a predicate indicating the presence of the other agent at a node, and $M = \{\texttt{left}, \texttt{right}\}$ represents the potential moves the agent may make. During each synchronous step, depending upon its current state, the answer to a query for the presence of the other agent, the agent uses δ in order to change its state and either move across the edge labeled $\texttt{left}$ or $\texttt{right}$. We assume that the agent halts once it detects the presence of the other agent at a node.

The first question one may ask concerning this instance of rendezvous is whether or not it is solvable. It is fairly easy to see that if the two agents start at an odd distance apart on an even size ring they can never rendezvous in the above model as they are forced to move on each step and, therefore, will remain an odd distance apart forever. There are number of ways to fix this, the easiest perhaps, being to add a third option to M of $\texttt{stay}$. Another option is to allow for the possibility of rendezvous on an edge. For simplicity in the analysis below, we will sometimes assume that they are an even distance apart on an even size ring. Even under these assumptions, we shall see that rendezvous is not always possible.

For solvable instances of rendezvous, one is interested in comparing the efficiency of different solutions. Much of the research focuses on the time complexity, the number of moves required to rendezvous or the expected number in the case of randomized agents (where the expectation is taken over the possible sequences of coin flips made by the agents). In some situations, it makes a difference if the agents begin their rendezvous procedure at the same time, or there is possible delay between start times. Here we will generally assume a synchronous start. Also of interest is the size of the program required by the agents to solve the problem or its memory requirement. Ideally one would like to design an agent whose size is constant independent of the size of the ring and which performs rendezvous in expected linear time (as in the worst case the agents are a linear distance apart initially). As we shall see, achieving both goals simultaneously is not always possible.

In the deterministic synchronous setting where the agents are anonymous, something is required to "break symmetry" as otherwise two agents starting in the same state will act the same forever and never rendezvous. One such symmetry breaking mechanism is the use of *tokens* (introduced in (14)) to mark a node on the ring (e.g., the starting position of the agent). Depending on the model, tokens may be *movable* or *stationary*, i.e., used to mark different nodes at different times or permanent marks once released. The tokens are generally assumed to be *indistinguishable*, i.e., tokens produced by different agents or the same agent at different times are identical. The number of tokens an agent may use in an algorithm is a measure of the amount of memory provided by the nodes of the network and becomes another potential resource to be studied.

1.4   OUTLINE OF THE BOOK

The focus of this monograph is on providing a rigorous introduction to understanding the rendezvous search problem in the distributed computing setting by proposing and analyzing various algorithms for various models and networks. For the most part, our investigations concentrate on the ring network. Chapter 2 discusses deterministic algorithms for rendezvous of two mobile agents using tokens while Chapter 3 studies the same problem for more than two agents. Chapter 4 focuses on randomized rendezvous. Chapter 5 discusses various other mobile agent models, including faulty and flickering tokens, the 'Look-Compute-Move' model, dangerous networks (black holes), and the relationship between rendezvous and the traditional problem of leader election. Chapter 6 considers rendezvous in various other topologies including tori, trees, and arbitrary graphs.

1.5   COMMENTS AND BIBLIOGRAPHIC REMARKS

There is extensive literature on the use of mobile agents in the distributed systems setting. The edited volumes of Milojicic et al. (78) and Weiss (94) are good places to start. The Nobel laureate T. C. Schelling is generally credited with introducing the rendezvous problem in his book (89) concerning the strategy of conflict and has been studied in many other settings besides the one considered here. For an excellent discussion of mainly continuous domains with randomized agents, see the book by Alpern and Gal (8). For work on robot rendezvous, consider (85) and (9) as possible starting points.

Of related interest is exploration, which is concerned with designing an algorithm for the agent that allows it to visit all of the nodes and/or edges of a given network (70; 35; 32).

CHAPTER 2

Deterministic Rendezvous in a Ring

2.1 INTRODUCTION

In this chapter, we study the rendezvous problem for two identical mobile agents in an anonymous, synchronous, and possibly oriented ring with n nodes. In our approach, the mobile agents do not use randomized algorithms or even different deterministic algorithms to break symmetry. Instead, although they run the **same** deterministic algorithm, they employ indistinguishable stationary or movable tokens placed at selected nodes of the ring in order to break symmetry and eventually rendezvous at a node.

First, we establish when identical stationary tokens cannot be used to break symmetry. We analyze the problem using two parameters:

1. the initial distance d between the two agents, and

2. the size (number of nodes) n of the ring.

We assume that d and n are even numbers. It is shown that rendezvous depends on the feasibility of breaking symmetry, which in turn, depends on whether or not $d < \frac{n}{2}$. Then we study the rendezvous problem given that $d < \frac{n}{2}$. Each MA places its stationary token on its respective starting node in the ring and begins to walk around the ring at the speed of one node per unit of time. It is assumed that the MAs know that the network is a ring and that $d < \frac{n}{2}$, but they do not necessarily know d, n, or the orientation of the ring.

Table 2.1 displays upper and lower bounds on the time complexity necessary for rendezvous of the two mobile agents that use indistinguishable stationary tokens provided they know that $d < \frac{n}{2}$. The lower bounds derived are "as strong as they can be" in the sense that they are valid under the assumption that the MAs have unbounded memory, while the upper bounds assume that the amount of memory is as listed in the last column of the table.

Surprisingly, if the MAs know either d or n, then the lower bound on the time complexity of the rendezvous problem is $\frac{3n}{4}$. If both d and n are unknown, however, then the lower bound on the time complexity increases to $\frac{5n}{4}$.

To establish the upper bounds on the time complexity, we present four solutions to the rendezvous problem provided that $d < \frac{n}{2}$ and identical stationary tokens are being used to break sym-

Table 2.1: Bounds on time complexity for rendezvous problem with two mobile agents at distance $d < \frac{n}{2}$ in an n node anonymous synchronous ring.

	Knowledge		Lower	Upper	Memory
n	d	Orientation	Bound	Bound	Requirement
Yes	Yes	Yes	$3n/4$	$3n/4$	$O(\log d)$
Yes	Yes	No	$3n/4$	$5n/6$	$O(\log d)$
Yes	No	Yes	$3n/4$	$3n/4$	$O(\log n)$
Yes	No	No	$3n/4$	$3n/4$	$O(\log n)$
No	Yes	Yes	$3n/4$	$3n/4$	$O(\log d)$
No	Yes	No	$3n/4$	$5n/6$	$O(\log d)$
No	No	Yes	$5n/4$	$5n/4$	$O(\log n)$
No	No	No	$5n/4$	$5n/4$	$O(\log n)$

metry. These solutions, with one exception, prove that the lower bounds in Table 2.1 are tight. The exception occurs when d is known but the orientation of the ring is unknown. The lower bound on the time complexity is $\frac{3n}{4}$, but the corresponding upper bound is $\frac{5n}{6}$.

While the results in Table 2.1 assume that the MAs know $d < \frac{n}{2}$, the solutions can be easily changed so that the MAs stop if $d = \frac{n}{2}$. It merely requires that each MA have memory $O(\log n)$. The last row in Table 2.1 represents the case where the MAs do not know n, d, or the orientation of the ring. The solution used to calculate the upper bound requires $O(\log n)$ memory and $\frac{5n}{4}$ time. Later, we present another solution for the case where the MAs do not know n, d, or the orientation of the ring, but this solution requires $O(\log \log n)$ memory and $O(\frac{n \log n}{\log \log n})$ time. While this algorithm suggests that the MAs' memory complexity can be reduced at the expense of a solution's time complexity, there are limits if we attempt to improve this memory trade-off. Namely, we prove that if the MAs have $O(1)$ memory and do not know n, d, or the orientation of the ring, then it is impossible to construct an algorithm that stops if a rendezvous is impossible and otherwise ensures a rendezvous.

This last result, plus the upper bounds stated earlier, imply that solving the rendezvous problem when the MAs have only $O(1)$ memory requires a change in the model. Suppose that the tokens are no longer stationary, i.e., anytime a MA encounters a token, it can move the token to an adjacent node. In this case, it is possible to give an algorithm which requires only $O(1)$ memory, which successfully uses indistinguishable but movable tokens to break symmetry and solve the rendezvous problem.

2.2   A SINGLE STATIONARY TOKEN

First, we propose and study algorithms whereby each mobile agent can employ only one stationary token to break symmetry in the rendezvous problem. Recall that the tokens employed are indistinguishable.

2.2.1   THE FEASIBILITY OF RENDEZVOUS

Before we provide algorithms that use identical stationary tokens to break symmetry in the rendezvous problem, we need to identify the conditions under which identical stationary tokens can be used to that end. The following examples clarify the dependence of the feasibility of a solution on the parity of the size of the ring and the existence of tokens.

Example 2.1   Consider an anonymous, synchronous and oriented ring with four nodes ($n = 4$) where two identical MAs, say A, B, are located at two different nodes distance two apart (see Figure 2.1). If the MAs are synchronous and run the same deterministic algorithm, they will never

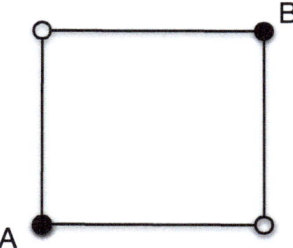

Figure 2.1: Two mobile agents at distance two from each other in a four-node ring.

be able to rendezvous since they move in the same direction, at the same speed, and at the same time. This difficulty cannot be resolved even in the presence of indistinguishable (stationary or movable) tokens.

Example 2.2   As another example, consider the rendezvous problem for two mobile agents on a three node oriented ring (see Figure 2.2). If there are no tokens available, the only way the two mobile agents can break symmetry is by "moving in opposite directions" along the vertices of the ring. This is not possible since they are identical and will always choose the same direction to move in. Rendezvous is guaranteed, however, if each MA has an identical stationary token that it leaves at its respective starting node. The algorithm directs each MA to walk until a token is reached, reverse direction, and continue walking until rendezvous occurs. Recall that agents will immediately detect the presence of another agent at a node. Rendezvous in this case will occur after just two steps; the

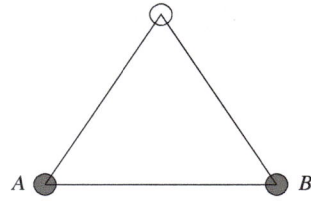

Figure 2.2: Two mobile agents at distance one from each other in a three-node ring.

reason is that, depending on the orientation chosen, one MA will encounter a token in two hops while the other in one hop.

Our first result is essentially a generalization of the first example, i.e., when n is even and $d = \frac{n}{2}$, it is impossible to provide an algorithm that uses identical stationary tokens to break symmetry and thus solve the rendezvous problem.

To make the proof rigorous we need to make precise the capabilities of the mobile agents. Let the atomic operations in the algorithms be restricted to the following:

RT: release the token

QT: query the host node to see if it contains a token

QMA: query the host node to see if it contains another MA

MCL: move one node clockwise

MCC: move one node counterclockwise

DM: do not move

$IC(count)$: increment the variable $count$ by one (if sufficient memory is available)

In addition to the atomic operations listed above, an algorithm may contain two constructs:

$do - until$ **loop:** the MA will repeat a finite sequence of operations until a given state occurs.

$if - then$ **statement:** if a given condition holds, the MA will perform a finite sequence of operations.

Using these formalizations, we can make precise what the mobile agents can do. The following two lemmata are necessary for the proof of the main feasibility result (Theorem 2.5).

Lemma 2.3   *Assume that the MAs are initially $d > 0$ nodes apart on the ring. If the MAs execute an identical algorithm from a common start time and that algorithm is restricted to a finite sequence of atomic* *operations, i.e., there are no do − until loops or if − then statements, then d, the distance between the mobile agents, will not change.*

Proof. Consider an algorithm comprised of just one atomic operation. Any one of the atomic operations $\{RT, QT, QMA, IC(c), DM, MCL, MCC\}$ will leave d unchanged, as either both MAs are stationary or each MA moves one node in the same direction. Assume that this is also true for an algorithm that is a sequence of k atomic operations.

Consider an algorithm that is a sequence of $k + 1$ atomic operations. Assuming that d is unchanged after k atomic operations, it will also be unchanged if the $k + 1$th operation is one of $\{RT, QT, QMA, IC(c), DM\}$ since the MAs are stationary under these atomic operations. The value of d is also unchanged if the $k + 1$th operation is one of MCL, MCC since the MAs move one node in the same direction. Thus d is unchanged after $k + 1$ atomic operations. This completes the proof of Lemma 2.3. □

Lemma 2.3 implies that if the two MAs begin an algorithm with distance $d = n/2$ and the algorithm contains only atomic operations, then the MAs will not rendezvous. A rendezvous cannot occur unless $do − until$ loops or $if − then$ statements are used. The inclusion of these constructs in an algorithm is a necessary but not sufficient condition for rendezvous.

Lemma 2.4 *Assume that the MAs are initially $d = \frac{n}{2}$ nodes apart on the network such that CLToToken = CCToToken = 0 for both MAs where, for a given MA, CLToToken and CCToToken denote the distance to the nearest token in the clockwise and counterclockwise direction, respectively. If time t^* is the first time during the algorithm that d is not equal to n/2, then t^* is also the first time that the MA's respective values for CLToToken (and thus CCToToken) differ.*

Proof. For all $t < t^*$, $d = n/2$ so that either both MAs are on separate tokens or neither MAs is on a token. If both MAs are on separate tokens, then $CLToToken = CCToToken = 0$ for both MAs. Suppose that at time t^*, neither MA is on a token. Suppose further that there exists a time $t' < t^*$ such that t' is the first time that the MA's respective values for $CLToToken$ differ, as do their respective values for $CCToToken$. Let $\{CLToToken_1, CCToToken_1\}$ and $\{CLToToken_2, CCToToken_2\}$ be the MA's respective values. Suppose, without loss of generality, that $CLToToken_1 < CCToToken_2$. If both MAs move $CLToToken_1$ nodes in the clockwise direction, then one MA will be on a token, but the other MA will not. Thus the distance between the MAs was not $d = n/2$. This contradiction proves Lemma 2.4. □

Consider the conditional statements that are part of the $do − until$ loop and the $if − then$ statement. The boolean values of these conditional statements determine, respectively, how many iterations of the loop occur or if the body of the $if − then$ statement is executed. In either case, a conditional statement to be evaluated at time t is a function of the known history of the given

MA at time $t - 1$. Two MAs cannot evaluate the same conditional statements at time t and receive different boolean values unless their known histories differ at time $t - 1$.

Theorem 2.5   (88).   *Consider two identical MAs in an anonymous n node ring (n even). The MAs are initially $d = \frac{n}{2}$ nodes apart on the network. To begin, each MA places an indistinguishable token on its respective starting node and these tokens remain in place for the rest of the algorithm. The two MAs will never rendezvous if they use the same deterministic algorithm.*

Proof.   A MA's state includes its values of *CLToToken* and *CCToToken*. Let s_0^i represent the ith MA's state at time 0. The ith MA's history at time t is defined as the sequence $H_t^i = s_0^i, s_1^i, ..., s_t^i$.

Suppose that the two MAs rendezvous at time t. This implies that at time $t, d = 0$. Consider the first time, $t^* < t$, that d is not equal to $n/2$. Lemma 2.4 implies that this will also be the first time that, respectively, *CLToToken* and *CWToToken* are not equal for the two MAs. At time t^*, d (and thus *CLToToken* and *CCToToken*) changes because either:

1. one MA executed DM and the other MA executed MCL or MCC so that d changed by one

2. one MA executed MCL and the other MA executed MCC so that the distance changed by two.

Since d changed at time t^*, the MAs necessarily executed conditional statements at that time and received different values. This implies that the histories of the MAs differed at time $t^* - 1$. Let time $t' \leq t^*$ denote the first time that the histories of the MAs differ. If the histories of the MAs first differ at time t', then Lemma 2.3 implies that a single atomic operation will leave the states unchanged. The states at time t' could differ only if a conditional statement evaluated at that time yielded different values for the two MAs, which implies that the histories of the MAs differed at time $t' - 1$. This contradicts the fact that t' was the first time that the histories differed.   □

2.2.2   THE TIME COMPLEXITY OF RENDEZVOUS

While Theorem 2.5 proves that identical stationary tokens cannot be used to break symmetry when $d = \frac{n}{2}$, Theorems 2.6 and 2.7 below provide the lower and upper bounds for time complexity of the rendezvous problem when symmetry can be broken using identical stationary tokens, i.e., $d < \frac{n}{2}$.

Theorem 2.6   (71).   *Consider two identical MAs at distance $d < \frac{n}{2}$ from each other in an anonymous, synchronous, ring having n nodes. The MAs know that $d < \frac{n}{2}$ and that the network is a ring. The MAs are assumed to have unbounded memory. When the MAs simultaneously run the same deterministic algorithm for the rendezvous problem, the lower bounds stated in Table 2.1 hold.*

Proof. **(Outline)** Consider the case where the MAs know d. After a MA travels d nodes in a given direction from its starting node, it has new information because it either finds a token or learns that the token is in the other direction from the starting node. The MAs are still at least d nodes apart, however, so a rendezvous requires that the MAs travel at least another $\frac{d}{2}$ nodes. Therefore, since the MAs must travel at least $\frac{3d}{2}$ nodes for a rendezvous to occur and moving to an adjacent node takes one unit of time, a rendezvous requires at least $\frac{3d}{2}$ units of time. In the worst case $d = \frac{n}{2} - 1$, and rendezvous requires at least $\frac{3n}{4} - O(1)$ units of time. This proves the lower bound for all cases where d is known.

Now assume that the MAs do not know d but they know n, the number of nodes in the ring. One of the MAs may find a token after travelling d nodes in a given direction. The other MA, however, might not have any new information until it travels $\frac{n}{2}$ nodes in the same direction. At that time, the MAs will still be at least d nodes apart. Given that the MAs must travel at least $\frac{n+d}{2}$ nodes for a rendezvous to occur, and moving to an adjacent node takes one unit of time, then a rendezvous requires at least $\frac{n+d}{2}$ units of time. Thus, taking $d = \frac{n}{2} - 1$, rendezvous requires at least $\frac{3n}{4} - O(1)$ units of time. This proves the lower bound for all cases where n is known.

In the remaining cases, the MAs know neither n nor d. A MA can count m, the number of nodes from its starting node to the first token, but it cannot tell if $m = d$ or $m = n - d$ until it has travelled around the entire ring and counted n. When the MAs return to their respective starting nodes, they are still d nodes apart. Given that the MAs must travel at least $n + \frac{d}{2}$ nodes for a rendezvous to occur, and moving to an adjacent node takes one unit of time, then a rendezvous requires at least $n + \frac{d}{2}$ units of time when n and d are unknown. Taking $d = \frac{n}{2} - 1$, shows that a rendezvous requires at least $\frac{5n}{4} - O(1)$ units of time in the worst case. This proves the lower bound for all cases where n and d are unknown. $\qquad\square$

The upper bounds for the time complexities stated in Table 2.1 are proved in Theorem 2.7 below. They are derived by designing an algorithm that ensures a rendezvous under the given conditions, e.g., Algorithm 1 ensures a rendezvous when d and the orientation of the ring are known but n is not necessarily known. While the calculation of the lower bounds in Theorem 2.6 assumes that the MAs have unbounded memory, the memory requirements for the upper bounds are those of the corresponding case, e.g., the case of Algorithm 1 requires $O(\log d)$ memory for each MA.

Before giving the proof of Theorem 2.7, we discuss the resulting complexity bounds implied by the algorithms presented during the course of the proof. In particular, with the exception of the case where d is known and the ring is not oriented, the lower bounds of Theorem 2.6 are tight. Algorithms 1, 2, and 3 show that, with one exception, if the MAs know either d or n, the upper bound for the time complexity is $\frac{3n}{4}$. The exception occurs when d is known but the orientation of the ring is unknown. The upper bound, in this case is given by Algorithm 2 and is $\frac{5n}{6}$.

Theorem 2.7 (71). *Consider two identical MAs at distance $d < \frac{n}{2}$ from each other in an anonymous synchronous n node ring. The MAs know that $d < \frac{n}{2}$ and that the network is a ring. When the MAs* *simultaneously run the same deterministic algorithm for the rendezvous problem, the upper bounds stated in Table 2.1 hold.*

Proof. The proof of the upper bounds are based on four simple algorithms that we present in the sequel. These involve four cases depending on the relative sizes of the parameters d, n as well as the knowledge the mobile agents have about them. In the following cases, the MAs know that $d < \frac{n}{2}$ even if d or n are unknown.

Algorithm 1 assumes $O(\log d)$ memory, d and orientation are known, and n might be known.

Algorithm 1

1: Release the token.
2: Begin walking around the ring in a counterclockwise direction.
3: **If** a token is found within d steps, continue walking in the same direction.
4: Otherwise, **if** no token is found by d steps, reverse direction and continue walking.

With d and the orientation known, one MA is guaranteed to find a token in d steps and continues walking in same direction. The other MA reverses direction after d steps and continues walking. Rendezvous occurs in time $\frac{3d}{2}$. Thus for $d < \frac{n}{2}$, the worst case is $\frac{3n}{4}$.

Algorithm 2 assumes $O(\log d)$ memory, d is known but orientation is unknown, and n might be known.

Algorithm 2

1: Release the token.
2: Choose a direction and begin walking around the ring.
3: **If** a token is found within d steps, continue walking in the same direction.
4: Otherwise, **if** no token is found by d steps, reverse direction and continue walking.

The worst case occurs when the MAs choose opposite directions and each walks d steps without reaching a token. For $d < \frac{n}{3}$, the MAs reverse direction after d steps and continue walking. At time $2d$, each MA is back at its starting node so rendezvous occurs in another $\frac{d}{2}$ steps and thus the total number of steps is $\frac{5d}{2}$. With $d < \frac{n}{3}$, the rendezvous occurs in time at most $\frac{5n}{6}$. If $\frac{n}{3} \leq d < \frac{n}{2}$, however, then MAs will rendezvous at or before d steps, so that the rendezvous takes $\frac{n-d}{2}$ steps or at most $\frac{n}{3}$ steps. Thus for $d < \frac{n}{2}$, the worst case is $\frac{5n}{6}$.

Algorithm 3 assumes $O(\log n)$ memory, n is known, d is unknown, and orientation might be known.

In the worst case, the two MAs walk in the same direction. One MA walks d steps, finds a token, and continues walking in the same direction. The other MA walks $n/2$ steps, finds no token,

---

Algorithm 3

1: Release the token.
2: Choose a direction and begin walking around the ring.
3: **If** a token is found within $\frac{n}{2}$ steps, continue walking in the same direction.
4: Otherwise, reverse direction at $\frac{n}{2}$ steps and continue walking.

---

and thus reverses direction and continues walking. As a result, rendezvous occurs in time $\frac{n+d}{2}$ which, with $d < \frac{n}{2}$, is less than $\frac{3n}{4}$.

Algorithm 4 assumes $O(\log n)$ memory, orientation might be known, but d and n are unknown.

Algorithm 4

1: Release the token.
2: Choose a direction and begin walking around the ring.
3: Count the number of steps to the first token, δ_1, and continue walking.
4: Count the number of steps to the second token, δ_2.
    /* The MA is back at its starting node.*/
5: **If** $\delta_1 < \delta_2$, continue walking in the same direction.
6: Otherwise, reverse direction and continue walking.

The two MAs walk the same direction and thus rendezvous in $n + \frac{d}{2}$ steps which, with $d < \frac{n}{2}$, is less than $\frac{5n}{4}$. This completes the proof of Theorem 2.7. $\qquad\square$

The preceding algorithms assume that the MAs know $d < \frac{n}{2}$. Note that if any of these algorithms is run on an even size ring with $d = \frac{n}{2}$, the result would be an infinite computation. This problem is easily fixed. Suppose that in all cases, the MAs have $O(\log n)$ memory. The MAs can now count the number of steps taken after they make a decision whether or not to change direction. For example, in Algorithm 2, the MAs make a decision whether or not to change direction in step 3 or 4. If rendezvous does not occur in the next $\frac{3d}{2} \leq \frac{3n}{4}$ steps, then rendezvous is impossible and the MAs should stop. With $O(\log n)$ memory, therefore, the MAs no longer need to know if $d < \frac{n}{2}$.

This motivates the following distinction between two types of rendezvous: *rendezvous without detection* (also simply *rendezvous*, abbreviated $\mathcal{RP}$) and *rendezvous with detection* (abbreviated $\mathcal{RD}$). In the former case, the agents know that the rendezvous problem has a solution either for the given system configuration, or regardless of the system configuration, and they just want to accomplish rendezvous at a node of the ring in, say, minimum number of steps. (For example, in an odd size ring, the rendezvous problem is always solvable for two mobile agents.) In the latter case, we are also interested in the decision problem, which in addition to rendezvous, requires a solution of the *halting problem* for rendezvous, I.e., an algorithm that detects feasibility of a solution for all starting positions after a *finite number of steps* (usually dependent either on their distance or the size of the network). Thus, if rendezvous is possible, then rendezvous is achieved, while if rendezvous is not possible, then all agents stop and know that rendezvous is not possible.

2.2.3   MEMORY TRADEOFF FOR RENDEZVOUS WITH DETECTION

With $O(\log n)$ memory, the solutions in Algorithms 1 to 4 can detect if $d = \frac{n}{2}$ and act appropriately, i.e., stop if $d = \frac{n}{2}$ and rendezvous otherwise. In Algorithm 4, where the MAs did not know n, d, or the orientation of the ring, the time complexity of the solution is $\frac{5n}{4}$. When the knowledge of the MAs is unchanged but their memory is reduced to $O(\log \log n)$, the following algorithm can detect if $d = \frac{n}{2}$ and act appropriately. The time complexity of the algorithm is

$$
O\left(\frac{n \log n}{\log \log n} \right),
$$

which suggests that the MAs' memory size can be reduced at the expense of a solution's time complexity. In the algorithm below, we assume that $p_1, \ldots, p_k$ denote the first k prime numbers such that $\prod_{i=1}^{k} p_i > n$.

Algorithm 5

1: Release the token.
2: Set $m = p_1$.
3: Choose a direction and begin traveling around the ring.
4: Count the number of steps, modulo m, to the first token, δ_1, and continue walking.
5: Count the number of steps, modulo m, to the second token, δ_2.
   /* The MA is back at its starting node. */
6: **If** $\delta_1 \bmod m = \delta_2 \bmod m$,
   If $m = p_k$, stop.
   /* Rendezvous is not possible. */
   If $m < p_k$, set $m = p_{i+1}$ and repeat from step 4.
7: **If** $\delta_1 \bmod m < \delta_2 \bmod m$, continue travelling in the same direction.
8: **Else** reverse direction and continue travelling.
   /* If step 7 or 8 is executed, rendezvous occurs in another $\frac{d}{2}$ steps.*/

Theorem 2.8 (71).   *Consider two identical MAs with memory $O(\log \log n)$ that are distance d from each other in an anonymous, synchronous n node ring. The MAs do not know n, d, the orientation of the ring, or if $d = \frac{n}{2}$. The MAs simultaneously run the same deterministic algorithm. In the rendezvous problem for two such MAs, Algorithm 5 correctly detects if $d = \frac{n}{2}$ and acts appropriately, i.e., stops if $d = \frac{n}{2}$ and rendezvous otherwise. The time complexity of the algorithm is $O\left(\frac{n \log n}{\log \log n} \right)$.*

Proof. The Chinese Remainder Theorem implies that if $d \equiv (n - d) \bmod p_i$ for all p_i, $i = 1, \ldots, k$, then

$$d \equiv (n - d) \bmod \prod_{i=1}^{k} p_i.$$

The algorithm checks each p_i in turn to see if $d \equiv (n - d) \bmod p_i$. If the statement is true for all p_i, then $d = n - d = \frac{n}{2}$ and the algorithm stops since rendezvous is impossible. If

$$d \not\equiv (n - d) \bmod \prod_{i=1}^{k} p_i,$$

for some p_i, however, then $d < \frac{n}{2}$. The first time the algorithm discovers such a p_i, one of the MAs reverses its direction and a rendezvous occurs $\frac{d}{2}$ steps later.

The worst case occurs when $d = \frac{n}{2}$ since all k of the p_i values have to be checked. The resulting run time is $O(kn)$, but we need to determine the value of k. Consider the smallest k such that $\prod_{i=1}^{k} p_i > n$. This implies that $\prod_{i=1}^{k-1} p_i \leq n$ and thus

$$\prod_{i=1}^{k} p_i \leq n * p_k \leq n^2.$$

Let $\Pi(m)$ denote the number of prime numbers less than or equal to m. (10) states that for any integer m,

$$\frac{m}{6 \log m} \leq \Pi(m) \leq \frac{8m}{\log m}.$$

Since p_i is prime by definition, $\Pi(p_i) = i$ for all i so that

$$\frac{p_i}{6 \log p_i} \leq \Pi(p_i) = i \leq \frac{8 p_i}{\log p_i}$$

and thus $p_i \geq \frac{i \log p_i}{8}$. Taking the product over all i and using Stirling's approximation (23) results in

$$\begin{aligned}
n^2 \geq \prod_{i=1}^{k} p_i &\geq \prod_{i=1}^{k} \frac{i \log p_i}{8} \\
&= k! 8^{-k} \prod_{i=1}^{k} \log p_i \\
&\geq k! 8^{-k} \\
&\geq 2^{\Omega(k \log k)}.
\end{aligned}$$

Taking the logarithms in the equation above, indicates that $2 \log n \geq k \log k$, so a valid value for k must satisfy $k \log k \leq 2 \log n$ and thus taking

$$k \in O \left(\frac{\log n}{\log \log n} \right)$$

is sufficient. Since the time complexity of the algorithm is $O(kn)$, we obtain the time bound $O(\frac{n \log n}{\log \log n})$. □

2.2.4   LIMITS TO THE MEMORY TRADE-OFF

While the results and discussion in section 2.2.3 imply that the MAs' memory size can be reduced at the expense of a solution's time complexity, the following theorem proves that there are limits in attempting to exploit this trade-off when the mobile agents have constant memory.

Theorem 2.9 (71).   *Consider two identical MAs with memory $O(1)$ that are distance d from each other in an anonymous, synchronous n node ring. The MAs do not know n, d, the orientation of the ring, or if $d = \frac{n}{2}$. The MAs simultaneously run the same deterministic algorithm. To begin an algorithm, each MA places an identical token on its respective starting node, and these tokens remain in place for the rest of the algorithm. No algorithm exists such that the MAs always correctly detect if $d = \frac{n}{2}$ and act appropriately, i.e., stop if $d = \frac{n}{2}$ and rendezvous otherwise.*

Proof. **(Outline)** Suppose there exists an algorithm such that the MAs can always correctly determine if $d = \frac{n}{2}$ and act accordingly, i.e., stop or rendezvous as appropriate. Consider a unidirectional ring of n nodes where $d = \frac{n}{2}$. With memory $O(1)$, each MA can store some constant k bits at a given time. These k bits represent the state of the MA at the given time and the MA's next action is determined by this state. Randomly, select one of the MAs and denote it as MA_1.

Construct the following sequence of bits for each node in the ring. The first k bits in the sequence are those stored in MA_1's memory upon its first visit to the given node. On each subsequent trip to the node, the k bits stored in MA_1's memory at the time of the visit are appended to the sequence. Let R denote the number of complete trips around the ring completed by MA_1. The resulting sequence of bits for a given node will contain at least Rk bits. These Rk bits represent the history, i.e., the sequence of states, of MA_1 at the given node. In a ring with n nodes where n is sufficiently large, i.e., $n >> Rk$, two such constructed sequences of bits will be identical, i.e., two distinct nodes will have the same sequence of Rk bits. If n is large enough, these two nodes will not be separated by a token.

Let $node_a$ and $node_b$ denote the two nodes with identical bit sequences, where $node_a$ precedes $node_b$ in the unidirectional ring. By the construction of the bit sequences, MA_1 is in the same state at $node_a$ as it is at $node_b$ for *each* of the R complete rounds of the algorithm. If all of the nodes from $node_a$ up to, but not including, $node_b$ are removed from the ring, the behaviour of MA_1 at $node_b$ and any other remaining node is unchanged, i.e., the behaviour of the two MAs, under the given algorithm, is the same in the original ring where $d = \frac{n}{2}$ as in the altered ring where $d < \frac{n}{2}$. This contradicts the supposition that the algorithm stops without a rendezvous in the former case and ensures in a rendezvous in the latter case. Thus there is no algorithm that, for MAs with memory $O(1)$, always correctly detects if $d = \frac{n}{2}$ or $d < \frac{n}{2}$, and, respectively, stops or ensures a rendezvous. □

2.3 MOVABLE TOKENS

This section studies rendezvous with detection ($\mathcal{RD}$) using movable tokens and explores trade-offs between the number of tokens available to the agents and the time needed to rendezvous with detection on an n node ring. In particular, we include impossibility, upper and lower bound results for two mobile agents with constant memory and one or more movable tokens each in an n node ring. The main results for one and two tokens are summarized in Table 2.2. The first column depicts the number of tokens available per mobile agent, the second indicates the number of directions on the ring (1 means unidirectional and 2 bidirectional), while the third and fourth columns indicate the time required to solve the problem indicated. The symbol ∞ in the table under the column "Time required for rendezvous" indicates an impossibility result. The memory required for all the

Table 2.2: Time bounds for two mobile agents with constant memory to detect if rendezvous with detection is possible ($\mathcal{RD}$) and to rendezvous when input is asymmetric ($\mathcal{RP}$) on an n node synchronous uni-, bi-directional ring with one or two tokens.

Conditions		Time Required for Rendezvous	
# of Tokens	# of Directions	$\mathcal{RD}$	$\mathcal{RP}$
1	1	∞	∞
1	2	∞	$\Theta(n^2)$
2	1	$\Theta(n^2)$	$\Theta(n^2)$
2	2	$\Theta(n^2)$	$\Theta(n^2)$

algorithms depicted is $O(1)$. Due to the complexity of the proofs of the lower bounds, in this section, we present only the algorithms which establish the upper bounds. The interested reader can find details of the lower bound proofs in (24).

First, consider the case where each mobile agent has a single token and the ring is bidirectional. In this case, the asymmetric rendezvous problem is solvable, as shown in the following theorem.

Theorem 2.10 (24). *In bidirectional rings, the rendezvous problem ($\mathcal{RP}$) is solvable in $O(n^2)$ time for two mobile agents having constant memory and one movable token each.*

Proof. Before presenting the main algorithm, we recall a weaker movable token algorithm due to (71). Both mobile agents leave their token at their start position. Then each mobile agent repeats the following algorithm until the two tokens are placed by a mobile agent in the same node. Each agent walks until it finds the other agent's token; it lifts the token, reverses direction, moves it one node in the new direction, and walks until it finds the other token. Then it iterates the above procedure. The first mobile agent to place the two tokens together stops and waits for the other agent to rendezvous at that node. It is easy to show that this algorithm always works when the mobile agents are in an asymmetric configuration. However, it accomplishes rendezvous only in time $O(n^2 \log n)$, and this is tight (e.g., in a ring of even size consider the case of two mobile agents with starting distance $d = n/2 - 1$).

In the sequel, we modify this algorithm by adding a "test counter" that counts modulo 3 in order to detect changes to the relative position of the two tokens. The effect is to achieve rendezvous in $O(n^2)$ time.

Consider Algorithm 6 for a mobile agent.

Algorithm 6 (One-Token)

1: Drop your token at your home base.
2: Go right until a token is found or you meet the other agent, counting in the state the distance traveled modulo three. Let this distance be x (remember it in your state).
3: **if** not met the other agent
4:     **repeat**
5:         Reverse direction, pick the token, move one step and drop the token there.
6:         Continue in current direction until a token is found, counting distance traveled modulo 3. Let this distance be y.
7:     **until** $y \equiv (x - 1) \bmod 3$ or met the other agent
8:     **if** did not meet the other agent.
9:         Stop and wait for the other agent.
10:     **endif**
11: **endif**

First, note that if the agents have different notion of which direction is right, they will start moving towards each other and will meet in $O(n)$ time. Hence, it is sufficient to consider the case where the agents have the same sense of direction. Let us call the agents A and B and the initial distances between them be d and $n - d$, respectively (see Figure 2.3). Let $t_1, t_2, t_3, \ldots$ be the times when the agent A finds a token (i.e. t_i is the time when i-th iteration of the loop begins). Let $t_1', t_2', t_3', \ldots$ be those times for the agent B. Without loss of generality, assume that $d < n - d$ and set $\delta = (n - d) - d$. Note that $d = t_1 \equiv x_A \bmod 3$ and $n - d = t_1' \equiv x_B \bmod 3$. Observe that as long as $t_{i+1} < t_i'$, the agent B will move a token before the agent A arrives to it, and A will find the distance between the tokens has not changed. However, as $t_1 \neq t_1'$, it is easy to prove by induction that in each iteration the time difference $t_i' - t_i$ between the agents increases by δ, i.e. $t_i' - t_i = i\delta$. That means that after $\lceil t_1/\delta \rceil$ iterations $t_{i+1} \geq t_i'$. If $t_{i+1} = t_i'$, the agents meet over the token. Otherwise, the agent A arrives to the token before B had moved it, i.e. A traveled distance

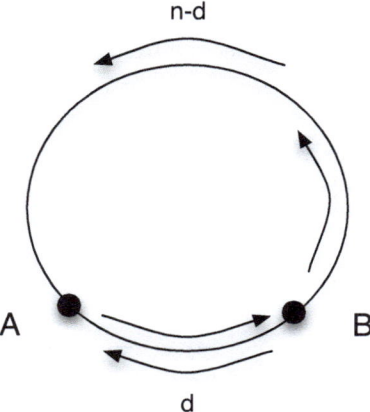

Figure 2.3: Determining the rendezvous time of two mobile agents at distance d from each other. Both agents start in the counterclockwise direction. Although agent A reached B's token and returns towards its original position, agent B has not yet found A's token.

$t_1 - 1 \equiv x_A - 1 \mod 3$. At that moment, A will stop and start waiting for B. As B has so far measured only equal distances, it will continue and eventually arrive at the place where A is waiting.

Since there are t_1/δ iterations of t_1 steps each, plus final time at most t_1' for the agent B to arrive to the meeting place, the rendezvous will happen in time $O((t_1/\delta)t_1 + t_1')$. Since $\delta \geq 1$, $t_1 < n/2$ and $t_1' = t_1 + \delta < n$, the resulting time is $O(n^2)$. □

Algorithm One-Token solves $\mathcal{RP}$ but not $\mathcal{RD}$, as it will run forever if the agents are initially in a symmetric configuration. Next, we show that rendezvous with detection can be solved if we endow each agent with two tokens, even in unidirectional rings.

Theorem 2.11 (24). *Rendezvous with detection (RD) is solvable in a unidirectional ring for two mobile agents with constant memory and two indistinguishable movable tokens each, in time $O(n^2)$.*

Proof. We present an algorithm (Algorithm 7) that at the cost of using two tokens per mobile agent detects the possibility of rendezvous and can eventually rendezvous when possible. Each mobile agent drops one token to its home node and the other token to the node located to its right. Then it travels right and moves every second token one position to the right (note that this will keep the home node tokens at their original locations). The process is repeated until the agent detects two tokens on top of each other. When this happens, it goes around and checks to see if the other two tokens are also on top of each other. If they are, then the home nodes were $n/2$ away, the whole computation was symmetric, and the agents can never rendezvous. If the other tokens are not on top of each other, then the agent waits as the other agent will eventually come to meet it.

Algorithm 7 (Two-Tokens)

1: Drop first token at your home base and second token to node located to the right.
2: **repeat**
3:      Travel right and move every second token you meet one position to the right.
4: **until** agent detects two tokens on top of each other.
5:      **if** two tokens are found on top of each other go around and check if other two tokens are also on top of each other.
6:          **if** yes then rendezvous is not possible **else** agent waits at last position.
7:      **endif**
8: **endif**

Let us divide the whole computation into rounds of n time steps each – during one round each agent completes a cycle around the ring and both second tokens are moved two steps. As the initial distance of the second token from the first token of the next agent is at most $d - 1 \leq n/2 - 1$, the worst case running time of this algorithm is bound by n times the number of rounds plus $n/2$ for the final check, resulting in $n((n/2 - 1)/2) + n/2$, which is in $O(n^2)$. This completes the proof of Theorem 2.11.   □

Observe that the unidirectional algorithm will trivially work (with the same bound on running time) in a bidirectional ring: If the agents have same sense of direction, they will run it as in unidirectional case, if they differ, they will start moving towards each other and meet in $O(n)$ time.

The next theorem provides a trade-off between number t of tokens being used and the time required for $\mathcal{RD}$. We consider the case of at least three movable tokens per mobile agent, i.e., $t \geq 3$.

Theorem 2.12   (24).   *Consider a synchronous ring with n nodes and two mobile agents located at two nodes of a bidirectional ring. Rendezvous with detection (RD) is solvable for two mobile agents having $t \geq 3$ tokens and $O(\log t)$ bits of memory each in time $O(mn)$, where m is the smallest integer such that $\binom{m-1}{t-2} \geq n - 1$.*

Proof. Suppose that each mobile agent has t tokens in its possession. A basic component of the proof is a counter, say C_t, that can count up to n. This is a segment of nodes of the ring delimited by two tokens at distance m, say, from each other. The values that this counter takes are held within this segment of nodes of the ring; one of the two tokens delimiting it is located at the home base of the agent while the other is the last token that the mobile agent released at a node of the ring at distance m from its home base.

Assuming that such counter exists, we can proceed just like in the proof of Theorem 2.11. The basic idea for $\mathcal{RD}$ is to have an agent go from its home base to the home base of the other agent, while incrementing its counter by one once in each round. After the counter is full, the agent continues to go from its home base to the base of the other agent but now decrementing its value by one once in each round. Notice that the counter can be incremented/decremented in time $O(m)$ per round. As with the algorithm of Theorem 2.11, when the counter reaches 0 before encountering its own home base, the mobile agent goes to the first base, and if the counter of the other mobile agent reaches exactly 0 at the second base as well, then the situation is symmetric and rendezvous is impossible: otherwise, wait at the second base in order to rendezvous with the other agent. Therefore, the algorithm just described not only accomplishes rendezvous but also detects whether or not it is possible. The running time of the algorithm presented will be $O(mn)$ since each round takes n steps which is the size of the ring.

Clearly, the running time of the algorithm is directly proportional to how compact the counter C_t can be, as the cost of moving is proportional to its size m, which is the distance between the two tokens delimiting the counter C_t. Therefore, for the given number t of tokens, it remains to determine m so that the mobile agent can implement a counter that can hold a maximum value n. By assumption, each mobile agent has t tokens. One token is being used to mark the mobile agent's home base thus leaving $t - 1$ tokens that can be used to implement the counter. The technical part is how to implement the counter, with the remaining $t - 1$ tokens. As depicted in Figure 2.4, the counter will be delimited by two tokens, located in nodes A, B, at distance m apart. A token is

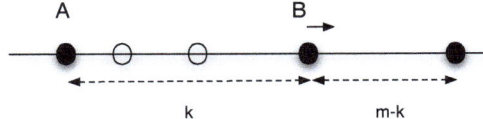

Figure 2.4: Incrementing a counter delimited by two tokens A, B at distance m from each other by changing the positions of the interior tokens. A is the home base (left delimiter) and B is the right delimiter of the agent. For example, the $t - 3$ interior tokens (depicted blank above) can be used to mark $\binom{k-2}{t-3}$ values of the counter. Depicted in the picture is k, the current length of the counter, and m, the longest length required, so as the counter C_t can count up to n, the size of the ring.

located at the home base A, say, of the agent. This leaves $t - 1$ tokens for marking positions at nodes of the network. Another taken located at B increments the range of the counter. Since the agent can count internally to $t - 1$ (since it has $t - 1$ tokens), all possible combinations of $t - 3$ tokens between two fencing tokens at distance k can be tried, and afterward increment k and repeat until the home base of the other mobile agent is reached, where $k \leq m$.

It remains to investigate what the size of the counter should be so as to guarantee that it is able to count up to n. For given k, there are $\binom{k-2}{t-3}$ possibilities (assuming no two tokens can lie on a single node, but appropriate combination numbers can be derived for that as well). Summing up over all $k \leq m$ until the home base of the other agent is reached results in at most

$$\sum_{k=2}^{m} \binom{k-2}{t-3} = \binom{m-1}{t-2}$$

possibilities (see (66)[page 56]). Since the position of the home base of the other agent is at most $n - 1$, the counter C_t needs to count up to $n - 1$. Therefore, the value of m will never need to exceed the smallest m such that $\binom{m-1}{t-2} \geq n - 1$. Further, notice that the two agents are required to have $O(\log t)$ bits of memory so that they can count internally up to t and thus distinguish the two delimiters of the counter C_t. This completes the proof of Theorem 2.12.   □

Elementary calculations show that the smallest integer m such that $\binom{m-1}{t-2} \geq n - 1$ is in $O(n^{\frac{1}{t-2}}t)$ and, therefore, the resulting running time for rendezvous with detection will be in $O(n^{\frac{t-1}{t-2}}t)$. As a corollary of Theorem 2.12 we obtain the following result.

Corollary 2.13   ((24))   *Rendezvous with detection (RD) is solvable for two mobile agents having $t > 2$ movable tokens and memory $O(\log t)$ each, in time $O(n^{\frac{t-1}{t-2}}t)$ in a bidirectional ring. Moreover, if $t = \log n$ then it takes time $O(n \log n)$.*

2.4   COMMENTS AND BIBLIOGRAPHIC REMARKS

Deterministic rendezvous algorithms for two agents in other settings (agents without tokens, asynchronous, arbitrary networks, etc.) are discussed in Chapters 5 and 6 and the references therein.

The rendezvous problem has also been extensively studied as a search game for two searchers placed in a continuous or discrete domain interested in minimizing the time required to rendezvous under assumptions as to the initial (probabilistic) distribution of the agents. Detailed investigations for this version of the problem can be found in (3; 5; 4; 6; 7; 13; 14) while (8) includes a book treatment of the subject.

Very little is known concerning lower bounds for agents with more than two tokens. However, for the case of unidirectional rings, we should mention the result of (24)[Theorem 7] relating rendezvous time with the number of tokens available by each agent. They show that the rendezvous problem $(\mathcal{RP})$ for two mobile agents having constant memory and t movable tokens each requires $\Theta(n^2/t)$ time in an unidirectional ring of size n.

CHAPTER 3

Multiple Agent Rendezvous in a Ring

3.1 INTRODUCTION

In this chapter, we study the rendezvous problem for $k \geq 2$ mobile agents carrying tokens, in a synchronous n node oriented ring. This problem is sometimes referred to as *gathering*. As was the case for two agents we first establish conditions under which the problem can be solved at all. We then provide solutions for the rendezvous with detection version of the problem (where the agents must eventually stop if they are in a situation where rendezvous is impossible) as well as algorithms for plain rendezvous (which can be shown to always stop assuming certain conditions hold such as primality of n, the ring size).

It turns out that rendezvous is only possible in the case where one of k or n is known. Since it is always possible to compute k given n or n given k using a single walk around the ring (i.e., an additional n steps), we present our algorithms assuming that k is known. Under these conditions, rendezvous is possible if and only if the sequence of inter-token distances is aperiodic.

We present three algorithms that solve the rendezvous with detection problem when k is known. The agents use one stationary token each. When $\mathcal{S}$, the sequence of inter-token distances between the MAs, is aperiodic, the algorithms guarantee that rendezvous occurs. However, if $\mathcal{S}$ is periodic and thus rendezvous is impossible, the algorithms guarantee that the MAs stop. We also

Algorithm	Memory	Time
8	$O(k \log n)$	$O(n)$
9	$O(\log n)$	$O(kn)$
10	$O(k \log \log n)$	$O(\frac{n \log n}{\log \log n})$
11	$O(\log n)$	$O(n)$
12	$O(\log k)$	$O(n)$
13	$O(\log k)$	$O(n \log k)$

Table 3.1: The Rendezvous problem with $k \geq 2$ mobile agents in a ring of size n.

present three algorithms that solve the rendezvous problem for values of k and n under various conditions (such as primality) that guarantee that the algorithms will halt. The memory and time complexities for these algorithms are also presented in Table 3.1.

It is worth mentioning that when solving the rendezvous problem with $k > 2$ agents, it can be shown that any algorithm requires at least $\Omega(\log \log n + \log k)$ memory ((54)).

3.2   IMPOSSIBILITY OF RENDEZVOUS

To solve the rendezvous problem, mobile agents must recognize when rendezvous is possible. As the next theorem indicates, knowledge of k or n is a necessary condition for the rendezvous of identical MAs in an anonymous, synchronous ring.

Theorem 3.1   (12).   *When each MA in the ring knows neither n, the number of nodes, nor k, the number of mobile agents, the mobile agent rendezvous problem is unsolvable.*

We refer the interested reader to (12)[Section 4, Theorem 2] for details of the proof. Even if k or n is known, it still may not be possible for the agents to rendezvous. Recall that two agents can not rendezvous on an even size ring when they are exactly $n/2$ nodes apart. Let $\mathcal{S} = d_1, \ldots, d_k$, be the sequence of inter-token distances assuming stationary tokens released at the starting positions of the agents. A sequence is *periodic* if it can be written as a $m > 1$ times repetition of a subsequence of $j \geq 1$ distances where both m, j divide k. It is possible to show the following result.

Theorem 3.2   (54).   *Assuming k is known, rendezvous is possible if and only if $\mathcal{S}$, the sequence of inter-token distances, is aperiodic.*

3.3   RENDEZVOUS WITH DETECTION

Given the results of section 3.2, the mobile agent rendezvous problem can be solved when the MAs can determine that $\mathcal{S}$, the sequence of inter-token distances, is aperiodic. Next, we consider algorithms for accomplishing rendezvous. The algorithms in this section assume an oriented ring.

First, assume that each MA has $O(k \log n)$ memory. The MAs know k but do not necessarily know n. As an immediate consequence of Algorithm 8, we can prove easily the following theorem.

Theorem 3.3   (54).   *If each MA has memory $O(k \log n)$, then Algorithm 8 solves the mobile agent rendezvous problem in time $O(n)$.*

If the MAs are restricted to memory $O(\log n)$, the mobile agent rendezvous problem is still solvable.

Consider Algorithm 9. In each round, a MA may become inactive and thus spend the rest of the algorithm at its starting node. Since the MAs share a common orientation and travel in the same direction, an active MA can identify an inactive MA because the former will find the latter

---

Algorithm 8

1: Release the token at the starting node.

2: Begin to walk around the ring in clockwise direction.

3: Compute the k inter-token distances $d_1, \ldots, d_k$.

4: **If** $S = d_1, \ldots, d_k$ is periodic, then stop. /* Rendezvous is not guaranteed. */

5: Set *forward* $= d_1, \ldots, d_k$ and *reverse* $= d_k, \ldots, d_1$

6: Let *lexi(someSequence)* denote the lexicographically maximum rotation of the sequence *someSequence*.

7: Set *forward* = *lexi(forward)* and *reverse* = *lexi(reverse)*.

8: **If** *forward* and *reverse* differ, then
i) determine which of these sequences is the lexicographic maximum and rendezvous at the node where this sequence starts.
ii) else let MA_i and MA_j denote the MAs at the beginning of *forward* and *reverse*, respectively.

9: **If** MA_i and MA_j are the same MA, then rendezvous at the node where MA_i resides.

10: **If** MA_i and MA_j are distinct MAs, then look at the two paths between MA_i and MA_j in the ring.
i) If only one of the paths had an odd number of nodes, then rendezvous at the node in the midpoint of that path.
ii) If both paths have an odd number of nodes, then a) if the paths differ in length, rendezvous at the midpoint of the shorter path, b) else compare the sequences of inter-token distances for the two paths and rendezvous at the node in the midpoint of the path that is the lexicographic maximum.
iii) If both paths have an even number of nodes, then walk clockwise, and if you are on the lexicographically minimal path, stop at its endpoint.

---

stopped. With only $O(\log n)$ memory, a MA needs more than one traversal of the ring to determine if S is aperiodic.

Theorem 3.4   (54).   *If each MA has memory $O(\log n)$, then Algorithm 9 solves the mobile agent rendezvous problem in time $O(kn)$.*

Algorithms 8 and 9 solve the mobile agent rendezvous problem when each MA has memory $O(k \log n)$ and $O(\log n)$, respectively. As indicated by Algorithm 10, it is also possible to solve the mobile agent rendezvous problem when each MA has memory $O(k \log \log n)$. Let $p_1, \ldots, p_r$ denote the first r prime numbers such that $\prod_{i=1}^{r} p_i > n$. As before, an active MA needs to recognize if another MA is active.

The following lemma is necessary for the proof of the main result in Theorem 3.6 below.

Lemma 3.5   *Consider a prime p such that $2 < p \leq r$. Assume that for all primes $p_i < p$, the sequence of distances mod p_i between the α_i active MAs is periodic such that $d_1, \ldots, d_{\alpha_i} \equiv (d_1, \ldots, d_{\alpha_i/a})^a \mod p_i$*

Algorithm 9

1: Release the token at the starting node.

2: Set $c = 1$. /* The number of the current round. */

3: Set $active = 1$. /* A bit to indicate whether the MA is active. */

4: Set $inactive = 0$. /* Count the number of inactive MA. */

5: Begin to walk around the ring in a clockwise direction.

6: Increment $inactive$ each time an inactive MA is met.

7: Compute the distance to the cth token, d_c, i.e., if $c = 1$, count the distance to the first token and if $c = 2$, count the distance to the second token, etc.

8: Continue to walk around the ring and compare d_c to each inter-token distance between the first and the last of $c + 1 \leq k$ consecutive tokens.

9: **If** MA sees an inter-token distance d_i such that $d_i > d_c$, then the MA continues in the same direction and becomes inactive, i.e., sets $active = 0$, when it reaches its starting node.

10: **If** MA did not see an inter-token distance d_i such that $d_i > d_c$, then the MA remains active when it returns to its starting node.

11: **If** only one MA remains active, i.e., $inactive = k - 1$, then walk around the ring and arrange the rendezvous. /* A MA that reaches this point is the sole active MA. */

12: **If** $c = k - 1$ and $inactive < k - 1$, then stop. /* All the inter-token distances are equal and thus rendezvous is impossible. */

13: **Else** set $c = c + 1$ and $inactive = 0$.

14: **Repeat** from step 5.

---

and $a \mid \alpha_i$. Let the first MA in each occurrence of the block $d_1, \ldots, d_{\alpha_i/a}$ remain active, while the remaining MAs become inactive. If the sequence of distances mod p between the a active MAs is periodic, then the original inter-token distances can be partitioned into $t \mid k$ equal length blocks with sums $\sigma_1, \sigma_2, \ldots, \sigma_t$ that are congruent modulo all the primes $p_1, p_2, \ldots, p$.

Theorem 3.6   (54).   *If each MA has memory $O(k \log \log n)$, then Algorithm 10 solves the rendezvous problem in time $O\left(\frac{n \log n}{\log \log n}\right)$.*

Proof. Algorithm 10 solves the rendezvous problem if it stops the MAs when rendezvous is impossible and otherwise ensures a rendezvous. Suppose that for all $p_i \leq p_r$, the sequence of distances mod p_i between the active MAs is periodic. Algorithm 10 will stop the MAs in step 9 and indicate that rendezvous is impossible. Lemma 3.5 implies that in the last round of Algorithm 10, where $p = p_r$, the original inter-token distances can be partitioned into $a_r \mid k$ equal length blocks with sums $\sigma_i^r, i = 1, \ldots, a_r$, that are congruent mod p for all $p \leq p_r$.

The Chinese Remainder Theorem then implies that the sums $\sigma_i^r, i = 1, \ldots, a_r$, are congruent mod $\prod_{i=1}^r p_i$. Since $\prod_{i=1}^r p_i > n$, then the original inter-token distances can be partitioned $a_r \mid k$

Algorithm 10

1: Release token at the starting node.
2: Set active = 1.
3: Set p_r to the first prime such that $\prod_{i=1}^{r} p_i > n$.
4: Set $p_i = p_1 = 2$.
5: Set $\alpha = k$, the number of active MAs.
6: Walk around the ring in a clockwise direction and compute the inter-token distances mod p_i between the α active MAs, i.e., $d_1, ..., d_\alpha$ mod p_i.
7: Set *forward* = $d_1, ..., d_\alpha$ mod p_i.
8: Set *reverse* = $d_\alpha, ..., d_1$ mod p_i.
9: **If** *forward* is periodic, i.e., *forward* = $(d_1, ..., d_{\alpha/a})^a$ mod p_i, then
   i) if at start of a block $(d_1, ..., d_{\alpha/a})$, remain active.
   ii) else set active = 0.
   iii) if $p_i < p_r$, then a) set $p_i = p_{i+1}, \alpha = a$, and repeat from step 6. b) else stop, since rendezvous is impossible.
10: **If** *forward* is aperiodic, then let *lexi(someSequence)* denote the lexicographically maximum rotation of the sequence *someSequence*.
11: Follow steps 7 through 10 of Algorithm 8.

into equal length blocks with sums σ_i^r that are equal for all $i, i = 1, \ldots, a_r$. This implies, however, that $n = a_r \sigma_i^r$ for any i and thus $a_r \mid n$. Since $\gcd(k, n) = g > 1$, $\mathcal{S}$ is periodic, and Algorithm 10 correctly stops the MAs in step 9.

Algorithm 10 must also guarantee that rendezvous occurs when possible, i.e., when $\mathcal{S}$ is aperiodic. Suppose not, i.e., $\mathcal{S}$ is aperiodic but rendezvous does not occur. This implies that for all $p_i \leq p_r$, the sequences calculated in step 7 of Algorithm 10 are periodic and thus all rounds of the algorithm will be executed. In the final round, where $p_i = p_r$, Algorithm 10 will stop the MAs and indicate that rendezvous is impossible. By the Chinese Remainder Theorem, however, this implies that $\mathcal{S}$ is periodic and thus contradicts the fact that $\mathcal{S}$ is aperiodic. Thus Algorithm 10 solves the mobile agent rendezvous problem.

If each mobile agent has memory $O(k \log \log n)$, then Algorithm 10 correctly determines whether rendezvous is possible and instructs the MAs to stop or rendezvous as appropriate. In the worst case, rendezvous is impossible and the MAs must complete all r rounds of Algorithm 10, where r is the smallest number of prime numbers such that $\prod_{i=1}^{r} p_i > n$. Each of the r rounds takes n steps so the time complexity is $O(rn)$. (71) proves that $r \in O(\frac{\log n}{\log \log n})$, so the time complexity of Algorithm 10 is $O\left(\frac{n \log n}{\log \log n}\right)$.   □

3.4   CONDITIONAL SOLUTIONS

In the preceding section, we gave algorithms for rendezvous with detection with different time/memory trade-offs. Under certain conditions, it is possible to improve upon these bounds by eliminating the need to check for situations where rendezvous is not possible. Such conditions arise for example when n is prime. A network designer or administrator may be able to choose the values of k and n so as to meet these conditions.

If $\gcd(k', n) = 1, \forall k' \leq k$, e.g., n is prime or is the product of two primes greater than k, then S_i is aperiodic for all i. Algorithm 11 assumes an oriented ring. An *active* token in unoccupied while an *inactive* token has a MA residing on it.

Algorithm 11

1: Release the token at the starting node.

2: Set $active = 1$.

3: Set $count = 0$.

4: Begin to walk around the ring in the clockwise direction.

5: Compute the inter-token distances to the next three active tokens, i.e., d_1, d_2, d_3, and increment *count* for each inactive token passed.

6: **If** $count = k - 1$, arrange rendezvous. (Only active MA remaining.

7: **If** $d_2 > d_1$ and $d_2 \geq d_3$, then remain active.

8: **Else** become inactive, i.e., set $active = 0$, continue in current direction to starting node, and wait for further instructions.

9: **Repeat** from step 3.

Theorem 3.7   (54).   *When the MAs share a common orientation and $\gcd(k', n) = 1$, for all $k' \leq k$, then Algorithm 11 solves the mobile agent rendezvous problem with $O(\log n)$ memory and in $O(n)$ time in an oriented ring.*

When k is prime, the ring is oriented, and $\gcd(k', n) = 1, \forall k' \leq k$, then a variation of Algorithm 11 solves the mobile agent rendezvous problem with $O(\log k)$ memory and $O(n)$ time.

Theorem 3.8   (54).   *When the MAs share a common orientation, k is prime, and $\gcd(k', n) = 1$, $\forall k' \leq k$, then Algorithm 12 solves the mobile agent rendezvous problem with $O(\log k)$ memory and in $O(n)$ time.*

Algorithm 13 solves the rendezvous problem when $\gcd(k', n) = 1$, $\forall k' \leq k$, but k is not necessarily prime.

Theorem 3.9   (54).   *When the MAs share a common orientation and $\gcd(k', n) = 1$, $\forall k' \leq k$, then Algorithm 13 solves the mobile agent rendezvous problem with $O(\log k)$ memory and in $O(n \log k)$ time.*

Algorithm 12

1: Release the token at the starting node.
2: Set active = 1.
3: **Begin** to walk around the ring in a clockwise direction.
4: Execute round 1 of algorithm 4 but calculate the inter-token distances mod k.
   /* All MAs will return to their starting nodes and those that became inactive have set active = 0. */
5: /* Now execute Algorithm 11 as if on a ring of size k The distances of interest are now the number of inhabited tokens between pairs of empty tokens. */
6: Compute the number of inhabited tokens, i.e., tokens hosting inactive MAs, met on the path to the next three uninhabited tokens, i.e., m_1, m_2, m_3.
7: **If** $m_1 = k - 1$, arrange the rendezvous.
   /* Only one active MA left */
8: **If** $m_2 > m_1$ and $m_2 \geq m_3$, then remain active.
9: **Else** become inactive, i.e., set $active = 0$, continue in current direction to starting node, and wait for further instructions.
10: **Repeat** from step 5.

Algorithm 13

1: Release the token at the starting node.
2: Set active = 1 and count = 0.
3: **Begin** to walk around the ring in the clockwise direction.
4: Compute the inter-token distances mod k to the next three active tokens, i.e., d_1, d_2, d_3 mod k, and increment $count$ for each inactive token passed.
5: **If** $count = k - 1$, arrange rendezvous.
   /* Only active MA remaining. */
6: **If** $d_2 > d_1$ mod k and $d_2 \geq d_3$ mod k, then remain active.
7: **Else** become inactive, i.e., set $active = 0$, and wait for further instructions.
8: **Repeat** from step 4.

3.5   COMMENTS AND BIBLIOGRAPHIC REMARKS

The rendezvous analysis for multiple mobile agents presented in this chapter first appeared in (54) and in the PhD thesis (88). An additional algorithm for multiple agent rendezvous can be found in (58) where optimal bounds on the memory requirements are shown. Multiple agent rendezvous algorithms in other networks and in other settings are discussed in Chapters 5 and 6 and the references therein. Teams of multiple mobile agents have also been used in other contexts and to solve other problems such as team theoretic decision making for efficiently searching unknown environments (84) and map exploration (29).

CHAPTER 4

Randomized Rendezvous in a Ring

4.1 INTRODUCTION

In this chapter, we consider the rendezvous problem on a synchronous, unoriented ring when the mobile agents' moves are random. First, we analyze the standard random walk for two mobile agents and compute the expected rendezvous time. Next, we look at how tokens can be used to reduce the expected rendezvous time. Finally, we establish an optimal time-memory trade-off for randomized algorithms when the agents do not use tokens. A summary of the results can be found in Table 4.1.

Table 4.1: Time-Memory Trade-offs for Randomized Rendezvous.			
Algorithm	**Time**	**Memory**	**Random Bits**
Random Walk	$O(n^2)$	$O(1)$	$O(n^2)$
Random Walk with Tokens	$O(n)$	$O(1)$	$O(1)$
Coin Half-Tour	$O(n)$	$O(\log n)$	$O(1)$
Approximate Counting	$O(n)$	$O(\log \log n)$	$O(n)$

The expected number of random bits used by an algorithm may be viewed as another resource of interest and is also included in the table. These values are easily derived from the descriptions of the algorithms.

Throughout this chapter, we model the agents as probabilistic finite automata $A = \langle S, \delta, s_0 \rangle$ where

- S is the set of states of the automata including s_0 the initial state and the special state `halt`, and

- $\delta : S \times C \times P \to S \times M$ where $C = \{H, T\}$ represents a random coin flip, $P = \{present, notpresent\}$ represents a predicate indicating the presence of the other agent at a node, and $M = \{left, right\}$ represents the potential moves the agent may make.

During each synchronous step, depending upon its current state, the answer to a query for the presence of the other agent, and the value of an independent random coin flip with probability of heads equal to .5, the agent uses δ in order to change its state and either move across the edge labeled left or right.

In the above model, one can easily see that if the two agents start at an odd distance apart on an even size ring, they can never rendezvous as they are instructed to move on each step and, therefore, will remain an odd distance apart forever. A way to fix this is to add a third option to M of stay. For simplicity in the analysis below, we will instead assume that the agents are an even distance apart on an even size ring.

4.2 RANDOM WALK ALGORITHM

Many people have noted that if two agents perform a random walk on a network they will eventually meet with probability one. This is the basis of the following algorithm for rendezvous of two mobile agents on an anonymous, synchronous, unoriented ring. The agents do not use tokens.

Algorithm 14 (Random Walk)

1: **Repeat until** other agent present:
2: **If** heads move right
    else move left

Its properties are summarized in the following theorem.

Theorem 4.1 (67). *Two agents with $O(1)$ memory each, starting at an even distance $d \leq n/2$ on an even n node synchronous and unoriented ring can rendezvous in expected $\frac{d}{2}(n - d)$ steps using the Random Walk Algorithm.*

Proof. If we let E_d be the expected time for two agents starting at an (even) distance d on an a ring of (even) size n to rendezvous using the above algorithm, it is easy to see that $E_0 = 0$, and $E_{n/2} = 1 + (1/2)E_{n/2} + (1/2)E_{n/2-2}$. The latter equation gives rise to the recurrence

$$E_{n/2} = 2 + E_{n/2-2}. \tag{4.1}$$

More generally, in executing the algorithm one of the following three cases may occur. The two mobile agents make a single step and either move in the same direction with probability 1/2, or in opposite direction either towards each other with probability 1/4 or away from each other with probability 1/4. From this, we derive the identity

$$E_d = 1 + (1/2)E_d + (1/4)E_{d-2} + (1/4)E_{d+2}, \tag{4.2}$$

for $d = 2, 4, \ldots, n/2 - 2$. (Note that the case $d = n/2$ is special in that they are always at most distance $n/2$ apart.) Substituting $d + 2$ for d in Identity 4.2 and solving the resulting equation in terms of E_d, we derive that for $d \geq 4$,

$$E_d = 2E_{d-2} - E_{d-4} - 4. \tag{4.3}$$

The initial condition $E_0 = 0$ and Identity 4.3 yield $E_4 = 2E_2 - 4$. More generally, we can prove the following identity for $2d \leq n/2$,

$$E_{2d} = d E_2 - 2d(d-1). \tag{4.4}$$

We prove by induction that there are sequences a_d, b_d such that

$$E_{2d} = a_d E_2 - 4b_d.$$

Indeed,

$$
\begin{aligned}
E_{2d} &= 2E_{2d-2} - E_{2d-4} - 4 \\
&= 2(a_{d-1}E_2 - 4b_{d-1}) - (a_{d-2}E_2 - 4b_{d-2}) - 4 \\
&= (2a_{d-1} - a_{d-2})E_2 - 4(2b_{d-1} - b_{d-2} + 1),
\end{aligned}
$$

which gives rise to the recurrences $a_d = 2a_{d-1} - a_{d-2}$ and $b_d = 2b_{d-1} - b_{d-2} + 1$ with initial conditions $a_0 = b_0 = 0$, $a_1 = 1$, $b_1 = 0$. Solving the recurrences we obtain easily that $a_d = d$ and $b_d = -\frac{1}{2}d + \frac{1}{2}d^2$, which proves Identity 4.4. To derive a formula for E_{2d}, it remains to compute E_2. Identity 4.4 yields the values

$$
\begin{aligned}
E_{n/2} &= \frac{n}{4}E_2 - 2\frac{n}{4}\left(\frac{n}{4} - 1\right) \\
E_{n/2-2} &= \left(\frac{n}{4} - 1\right)E_2 - 2\left(\frac{n}{4} - 1\right)\left(\frac{n}{4} - 2\right),
\end{aligned}
$$

which when substituted into Identity 4.1 shows that $E_2 = n - 2$. Finally, substituting this last value into Identity 4.4 we derive

$$E_{2d} = d(n - 2d). \tag{4.5}$$

Obviously the above algorithm translates into a finite automaton with a constant number of states and thus the proof of the theorem is complete. $\qquad \square$

The agents in this algorithm are of optimal (to within a multiplicative constant) size but in the worst case $d = \Theta(n)$ and the expected number of steps is quadratic. One might ask if it is possible to achieve linear time rendezvous.

4.3   RANDOMIZATION AND TOKENS

Having seen how the mobile agent rendezvous problem can be solved using randomization, it is worthwhile investigating how tokens and randomization can be combined to solve the problem. Suppose that the two MAs have memory $O(1)$ and know neither n nor d. We can prove the following theorem.

Theorem 4.2   (88).   *Two agents with $O(1)$ memory each, starting at an even distance $d \leq n/2$ on an even n node synchronous and unoriented ring and carrying one stationary token each can rendezvous in $O(n)$ expected time using Algorithm 15.*

Algorithm 15 (Random Walk with Tokens)

1: Release the token.
2: Set count = 0.
3: Choose a direction and walk until a token is reached.
4: At the token, set count = count + 1.
5: **If** count mod 2 = 0, change direction with probability $0 \leq p \leq 1$.
6: Otherwise, maintain the same direction.
7: Walk to the next token.
8: **Repeat** from step 4 until rendezvous occurs.

Proof. The expected number of rounds of Algorithm 15 is

$$\sum_{i=1}^{\infty} (2p(1-p))(1-2p(1-p))^{i-1}i = \frac{1}{(2p(1-p))}.$$

All but the final round take time n. Once the MAs are travelling in opposite directions on the ring, the expected time to rendezvous is $\frac{n}{2}$. Thus the total expected time to rendezvous is

$$n\left(\frac{1}{2p(1-p)} - 1\right) + \frac{n}{2} = \frac{n(1-p(1-p))}{2p(1-p)}$$

which is $O(n)$. The expected time is minimized when $p = \frac{1}{2}$. This completes the proof of Theorem 4.2. □

4.4   TIME/MEMORY TRADE-OFFS

We have seen in the previous section that by combining random walk with tokens, we managed to achieve a linear (on the number of ring's nodes) expected number of steps for rendezvous, while keeping the agents' size a constant. In this section, we are interested to see what is the optimal memory algorithm one can get, for achieving rendezvous between two agents in a synchronous, unoriented ring of n nodes within an $O(n)$ expected time, when the agents do not use tokens (i.e., exactly as in Section 4.2).

4.4.1   COIN HALF TOUR ALGORITHM

It is fairly easy to achieve a linear upper bound on the expected number of steps using Algorithm 16, referred to as the "Coin Half Tour" Algorithm in (3).

Theorem 4.3   (3).   *Two agents with $O(\log n)$ memory each, starting at an even distance $d \leq n/2$ on an even n node synchronous and unoriented ring can rendezvous in expected $O(n)$ steps using Algorithm 16.*

Algorithm 16 (Coin Half Tour)

1: **Repeat until** other agent present:
2: **If** heads move right for $n/2$ steps
   else move left for $n/2$ steps

Proof. If we refer to each execution of step 2 as a phase and consider a phase to be a success if the two agents choose to travel in opposite directions and a failure otherwise, then it is easy to see that (a) the expected number of failed phases before obtaining a success is one (b) the number steps in a failed steps is $n/2$ and (c) the number of steps in a successful phase is less than n. Therefore, the expected number of steps, until the agents rendezvous is $O(n)$ since they are guaranteed to rendezvous on a successful phase. Note that this is independent of their starting positions assuming $d > 0$. Further note that a finite automaton implementing the above algorithm requires $n/2 + O(1)$ states and thus the theorem has been proved. □

The above algorithm is optimal (to within a multiplicative constant) in its running time but requires $O(\log n)$ bits of memory. Is it possible to achieve linear running time with less memory?

4.4.2 APPROXIMATE COUNTING ALGORITHM

By replacing the exact $n/2$ steps taken in step 2 of the Coin Half Tour Algorithm with an approximate expected $O(n)$ steps, one can reduce the memory requirements for rendezvous in this instance. Consider Algorithm 17 for two agents with k bits of memory each.

Algorithm 17 (Approximate Counting)

1: **Repeat until** other agent present :
2: (a) **If** heads set $dir = $ right
          else set $dir = $ left
   (b) **Repeat until** 2^k heads observed in a row: Move in direction dir

---

By defining a phase correctly and with some analysis, it is possible to show that the phases have expected length $O(2^{2^k})$ and have constant probability of success and thus we can show:

Theorem 4.4 (69). *Two agents with k bits of memory each, starting at an even distance $d \leq n/2$ on an even n node synchronous and unoriented ring can rendezvous in expected*

$$O\left(\frac{n^2}{2^{2^k}} + 2^{2^k}\right)$$

steps using Algorithm 17.

In particular, the above theorem implies that with $\log \log n$ bits of memory rendezvous can be achieved in linear time. It turns out that this is optimal as it can be shown that:

Theorem 4.5 **(69).** *Any algorithm that achieves rendezvous between two agents in expected $\Theta(n)$ steps on an n node synchronous and unoriented ring requires $\Omega(\log \log n)$ bits of memory.*

The model of computation for the lower bound represents a rendezvous algorithm A as a probabilistic finite automaton having t states. Each vertex of the automaton has two outgoing edges representing the two possible results of a coin toss and each edge e is labelled with a real number $\ell(e) \in [-1, +1]$. The edge label of e represents a step of length $|\ell(e)|$ with this step being counterclockwise if $\ell(e) < 0$ and clockwise if $\ell(e) > 0$. The two agents use identical automata and start in the same state. The rendezvous process is complete once the distance between the two agents is at most 1. This model is stronger than the model used for the upper bound, since the edge labels are no longer restricted to be in the discrete set $\{-1, 0, +1\}$ and the definition of a rendezvous has been slightly relaxed.

Proofs of these theorems are based on a detailed analysis of the approximate counting algorithm using the theory of martingales, stopping times, and Wald's Identity. Details can be found in (69).

4.5   COMMENTS AND BIBLIOGRAPHIC REMARKS

It is worth mentioning that the study of randomized rendezvous problem has its origins with none other than George Pólya, who enjoyed taking walks in the forest while thinking about mathematics. According to (2) (see also (59)), "One day while out on his walk he encountered one of his students strolling with his fiancée. Somewhat later their paths crossed again and even later he encountered them once again." Being embarrassed "...this caused him to wonder how likely it was that walking randomly through paths in the woods, one would encounter others similarly engaged" which led to his seminal paper (81).

Since that time many authors have observed that rendezvous may be solved by anonymous agents on an anonymous network by having the agents perform a random walk. The expected time to rendezvous can be shown to be a (polynomial) function of the (size of the) network and is related to the cover time of the network. See (80) for definitions relating to random walks as well as (22) for an analysis of the meeting time for random walks.

A different but interesting variant of the rendezvous problem for single bit messages in general graphs is considered by (76). Each vertex u repeats the following actions for ever: 1) selects one of its neighbors, say $s(u)$, at random, 2) sends 1 to $s(u)$ and 0 to its other neighbors, and 3) receives messages from all its neighbors. Rendezvous occurs between u and $s(u)$ if u receives 1 from $s(u)$. The authors obtain upper and lower bounds on the expected maximal number of "rendezvous" instances, in general, graphs as well as specific graphs, like rings, chains, and complete graphs. For additional details see (77).

CHAPTER 5

Other Models

5.1 INTRODUCTION

In this chapter, we continue studying the ring topology and begin with a proof of the equivalence between leader election and the rendezvous problem for a set of mobile agents when the ring is oriented. We then proceed to discuss several mobile agent models and establish conditions and algorithms for rendezvous when tokens either fail or flicker probabilistically. We also consider the asynchronous ring and the look-compute-move models. We conclude by examining the problem in so-called dangerous networks that may contain hostile nodes referred to as black holes.

5.2 LEADER ELECTION AND RENDEZVOUS

In this section, we address the question of the relationship between the rendezvous problem and the leader election problem among k (anonymous) mobile agents in a synchronous ring. The MAs have one stationary token each and enough memory to count inter-token distances. The leader election problem refers to the process of designating a single MA as the unique coordinator of a particular algorithmic task concerning the network and the set of MAs. It turns out that the aforementioned relationship between the two problems depends on whether the MAs share a common orientation. We can prove the following theorem.

Theorem 5.1 (54). *Consider $k \geq 2$ anonymous mobile agents in an anonymous and synchronous ring. They are equipped with one stationary token each and enough memory to count inter-token distances. If the MAs share a common orientation on the ring, then the leader election problem is equivalent to the rendezvous problem for those MAs. If the MAs do not share a common orientation, however, then the leader election problem is strictly more complex than the rendezvous problem.*

Proof. **(Outline.)** If the leader election problem can be solved, then the elected MA can travel around the ring and instruct all other MAs to meet at a particular node. Thus a solution to the leader election problem for MAs always implies that there is a solution for the corresponding mobile agent rendezvous problem.

However, a solution to the mobile agent rendezvous problem does not necessarily imply a solution to the leader election problem. Consider the case where $k = 2$ MAs reside on $n = 3$ node

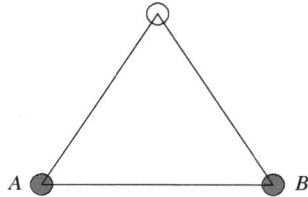

Figure 5.1: Two mobile agents at distance one from each other in an unoriented three-node ring.

ring (see Figure 5.1), k is known but the MAs do not share a common orientation.

Consider the rendezvous Algorithm 18. If the MAs move in the same direction initially (i.e.,

---

Algorithm 18

1: Begin to walk in the direction locally labelled **right**.
2: Walk until either:
   Step a. the other MA is met at a node, i.e., rendezvous occurs, or
   Step b. a token is discovered.
3: If a token is discovered, change direction and continue walking until rendezvous occurs.

---

the labelling is consistent), they will meet after two steps. If the MAs move in opposite directions initially, they will rendezvous after at most two steps. But in this case, leader election will not be possible as one MA cannot be distinguished from the other and their states can be shown to be identical throughout the execution of any algorithm. Thus when the MAs do not share a common orientation, the leader election problem for MAs is strictly more difficult than the corresponding rendezvous problem.

If the MAs do share a common orientation, however, then a solution to the rendezvous problem always implies a solution to the corresponding leader election problem. In Algorithm 10, the last MA that remains active organizes the rendezvous and that MA can be elected the leader. □

5.3   RENDEZVOUS WITH FAILING TOKENS

In this section, the model is extended to allow for token failure, i.e., when a token is no longer visible to any MA. For example, a token could fail if it is placed on a hostile node or if a malicious MA is able to flip the bit that represents the token.

Assume that n is the size of a synchronous unoriented ring. There are k MAs scattered on the ring. The MAs use one stationary token each, at most $k-1$ of which may fail, and $\gcd(k', n) = 1$ for all $k' \leq k$. Now the *inter-token distances* is the sequence of distances between the fault-free tokens, once they have been released. Since the tokens are stationary, the original inter-token distances are maintained unless a token fails. When a token fails, it is no longer visible to any agent passing by the node. We will consider two types of failures: when tokens can fail and thus disappear *upon their release* and when the tokens can fail *anytime*. We use f to denote the number of tokens that fail. As in our previous analyses, we will see that the complexity of the problem appears to depend upon the agents' knowledge of k and n. Concerning the feasibility of rendezvous, observe that if all tokens fail or if, k, the number of tokens, is such that $\gcd(k', n) \neq 1$ for some $k' \leq k$, then rendezvous is unsolvable in this model (see (54)).

5.3.1   RENDEZVOUS WHEN TOKENS FAIL UPON RELEASE

First, assume a token can fail only upon release, i.e., in the first step of a given algorithm. The agent that released the token is unaware that it failed. If neither n, the size of the ring, nor k, the number of agents, are known to the agent the problem is unsolvable (54); thus, in the following, we will consider two cases: when only n is known and when only k is known.

n KNOWN, k UNKNOWN

The algorithm is rather simple. Each agent releases its token, moves along the ring computing the distances between the successive tokens it encounters, and returns to its homebase. Let $s_1, \ldots, s_h$ be the sequence it computed, where s_1 and s_h are the distances between the homebase and the first encountered token, and between the last token and the homebase, respectively. If its own token did not fail, $h = k - f$ and this sequence is exactly the (circular) sequence $S = d_1, \ldots, d_h$ of the inter-token distances of the tokens that did not fail. If, however, the agent finds that its token has failed, then $h = k - f + 1$ and the agent must adjust the sequence to determine the actual (circular) sequence of inter-token distances: $S = d_1, \ldots, d_{h-1} = s_1 + s_h, s_2, \ldots, s_{h-1}$.

Since the failures happen before the agents start to move around, the circular sequence computed in this way is the same for all agents within a rotation (due to the fact that the ring is not oriented).

The agents will then agree on a meeting node by exploiting the asymmetry of the sequence (which cannot be periodic since $\gcd(k', n) \neq 1$ for all $k' \leq k$). More precisely, let S^R denote the reverse of S; each agent will compute the lexicographically maximum string in both S and S^R. If both strings start at the same node, that will become the meeting point; otherwise, the meeting point will be the midpoint in the odd path between the starting nodes of the two strings.

The routine that shows how to identify the meeting point, which will be used in all our algorithms, is described in Algorithm 19, where $lexi(someSequence)$ denotes the lexicographically maximum rotation of $someSequence$. The overall algorithm MEET1 is described in Algorithm 20. (Note that $m = k - f$ denotes the number of remaining tokens.)

The proof of the following theorem is straightforward.

Algorithm 19 MeetingPoint(string).

1: Compute $forward = lexi(string)$ and $reverse = lexi(string^R)$.
2: Let x and y denote the nodes at the beginning of *forward* and *reverse*, respectively.
3: If $x = y$, then x is the rendezvous point.
4: If $x \neq y$, then the rendezvous point is the midpoint of the odd path between x and y (such a path must exist because n is odd).

Algorithm 20 (MEET1)

1: Release the token at the starting node.
2: Choose a direction and walk once around the ring.
3: Compute the sequence of inter-token distances $s_1, \ldots, s_h$.
   If a token is present at this node: $\mathcal{S} = d_1, \ldots, d_m = s_1, \ldots, s_h$.
   If no token is present at this node: $\mathcal{S} = d_1, \ldots, d_m = s_1 + s_h, s_2, \ldots, s_{h-1}$.
4: Move to MeetingPoint($\mathcal{S}$).

Theorem 5.2 (53). *When the agents have $O(k \log n)$ memory, n is known, $\gcd(k', n) = 1$ holds for all $k' \leq k$, $f \leq (k-1)$ tokens fail, and tokens can fail only upon release, then the mobile agent rendezvous problem can be solved in less than $2n$ time units.*

Notice that, for this algorithm to work, the system does not need to be synchronous; in fact, each agent could independently make its calculations and move to the rendezvous point even if the ring is *asynchronous*.

k KNOWN, n UNKNOWN

More interesting is the case when n is unknown. As in the previous case, the agents will walk around the ring long enough to be able to calculate a sequence of inter-token distances; this sequence must be such that it covers the entire ring and contains an asymmetry that can be exploited by the agents to agree on a meeting point.

However, unlike the previous case, since n is not known, the circular sequences computed by the agents using solely knowledge of k, are not necessarily identical. In fact, each agent, to construct its sequence, will fully traverse the ring the same (unknown) number of times, but, depending on the starting point and on the number of failures, it will also traverse a portion of the ring, which is, in general, different for different agents.

Although the sequences are not the same, it can be shown that the agents can still identify an unique point where to meet by calculating $3k$ inter-token distances. The algorithm MEET2 is described in Algorithm 21.

Let $\mathcal{S}^{\mathcal{R}}$ denote the reverse of $\mathcal{S}$. Since the tokens fail only upon release, $\mathcal{S}^{\mathcal{R}}$ can be partitioned as follows:

$$\mathcal{S}^{\mathcal{R}} = Q^q + d_\gamma, \ldots, d_1, \tag{5.1}$$

where Q^q is the concatenation of q copies of a unique aperiodic subsequence Q, $+$ is the concatenation operator, and $d_\gamma, \ldots, d_1$ is a subsequence such that $\gamma < |Q|$. Upon identifying the subsequence Q, the agents can identify a unique node upon which to rendezvous.

Algorithm 21 (MEET2)

1: Release the token at the starting node.
2: Choose a direction and start walking.
3: Compute the sequence of $3k$ inter-token distances, i.e., $S = d_1, d_2, \ldots, d_{3k}$.
4: Let S^R be the reverse of S.
5: Find the shortest aperiodic subsequence Q that starts with the first element of S^R and is repeated such that $S^R = Q^q + d_\gamma, \ldots, d_1$ where $\gamma < |Q|$.
6: Move to MeetingPoint(Q)

Theorem 5.3 (53). *When the agents have $O(k \log n)$ memory, k is known, $\gcd(k', n) = 1$ holds for all $k' \leq k$, $f \leq (k - 1)$ tokens fail, and tokens can fail only upon release, then the mobile agent rendezvous problem can be solved in $O(kn)$ time.*

Proof. Let $m = k - f$ be the number of tokens that do not fail. Let $A = \delta_1, \ldots, \delta_m$ be the sequence of the m inter-token distances that exist after the f tokens have failed; clearly $\sum_{i=1}^{m} \delta_i = n$. Let $S(a)$ be the sequence of $3k$ inter-token distances calculated by a given agent a in step 3 of Algorithm MEET2. Let $S^R(a)$ be the reverse of $S(a)$ and A^R be the reverse of A. For all agents, the $3k$ inter-token distances are of the form

$$S^R(a) = (A^R)^\rho + d_\gamma, \ldots, d_1 = (\delta_m, \ldots, \delta_1)^\rho + d_\gamma, \ldots, d_1. \tag{5.2}$$

where $(A^R)^\rho$ is the concatenation of ρ copies of the aperiodic subsequence A^R, $+$ is the concatenation operator, and $d_\gamma, \ldots, d_1$ is a subsequence such that $\gamma < m$. Thus, there exists at least one aperiodic subsequence, namely A^R, that satisfies equation 5.1. Note that A^R is aperiodic as it has k or fewer inter-token distances, and by assumption $\gcd(k', n) = 1$ for all $k' \leq k$.

If A^R is the shortest subsequence that satisfies equation 5.1, the agents discover A^R in step 5 of Algorithm MEET2. Otherwise, the agents discover a shorter aperiodic subsequence, Q, that satisfies equation 5.1.

The subsequence discovered in step 5 of Algorithm MEET2 is unique. Here is why: If the shortest subsequence has z elements, these elements are the first z elements of S^R. Any other subsequence of the same length that satisfies equation 5.1 is also comprised of the first z elements of

S^R, and thus the subsequence discovered in step 5 is unique. This implies that all the agents identify the same rendezvous node in the remaining steps of Algorithm MEET2 and rendezvous occurs.

Calculating S, the sequence of $3k$ inter-token distances requires $O(k \log n)$ memory and requires $O(kn)$ time. Identifying the appropriate subsequence in step 5, determining the rendezvous node, and walking to the rendezvous node takes $O(kn)$ time, so the overall time requirement is $O(kn)$. This completes the proof of Theorem 5.3.   □

When the tokens only fail upon release, Algorithm MEET2 also solves the mobile agent rendezvous problem when the ring is *asynchronous*. Once an agent has calculated S^R, it can identify the smallest aperiodic sequence that satisfies equation 5.1. Since this sequence is unique, the agent can then identify the unique rendezvous node, walk there, and wait until all k agents arrive. The algorithm does not depend on timing but rather on the agents' ability to count and then identify the rendezvous node.

5.3.2   RENDEZVOUS WHEN TOKENS CAN FAIL AT ANY TIME

We now consider the situation when token failures can occur at any time. In this case, for the algorithms to work the system must be synchronous.

The idea is still to make use of the inter-token distances to agree on a meeting point. In this case, however, the problem is made much more complicated by the fact that these distances vary unpredictably during the algorithm. To cope with that, our algorithm works in rounds; in each round, the agents compute some inter-token distances and try to meet in a node. In a round, however, the rendezvous may fail because the agents might have computed different inter-token distances. In such a case, only groups of agents (the ones that have computed the same inter-token distances) might meet (in a "false" rendezvous point).

To make the algorithms work, the rounds must be synchronized so that the agents start them within some bounded time interval (if not simultaneously). In other words, an agent arriving at its meeting point will have to know how long to wait before declaring that point a false rendezvous point and correctly start the next round, or before realizing that such a point is a true meeting point.

n KNOWN *k* UNKNOWN

First of all, notice that since k is unknown, a group of agents finding themselves on the same node cannot determine whether rendezvous has been accomplished simply by counting how many they are. A different strategy will have to be used.

A round is composed of three distinct steps. In *step*1, an agent travels around the ring to compute the inter-token distances; it then identifies the lexicographical maximum string. In *step*2, the agent moves to the computed meeting point (let us assume that it takes t time units to go there), and it waits $n - t$ units to synchronize with the others for the next step. Notice that, in general, the agent cannot understand at this point if rendezvous is accomplished just by counting the other agents on the meeting node. As we will prove, if this is the third time that the same string has been calculated, the agent can be sure that this is a true meeting point. In this case, in fact, the agent knows that everybody else has seen this string at least in the previous and in the current rounds and is now in its own meeting point. $Step3$ is used for notifying all agents that indeed the meeting point is the correct one. The agents who know, go around the ring. The agents who do not know, wait for n units: if nothing happens, they go to the next round; if a notifying agent arrives, they terminate the algorithm. The algorithm MEET3 is described in Algorithm 22.

Algorithm 22 (MEET3)

1: Release token.
2: Set $S_1 = S_2 = S_3 = \emptyset$
3: Set $r = 0$, choose a direction and begin walking.
4: Travel for n time units computing the inter-token distances $S = (s_1, \ldots, s_h)$.
   If a token is present at the last node: $S = d_1, \ldots, d_m = s_1, \ldots, s_h$.
   If no token is present at the last node: $S = d_1, \ldots, d_m = s_1 + s_h, \ldots, s_{h-1}$.
5: Set $t = 0$.
6: Walk to $MeetingPoint(S)$ and increment t for each node traveled.
7: Wait $n - t$ clock ticks.
8: Set $S_1 = S_2$; $S_2 = S_3$; $S_3 = S$.
9: If $S_1 = S_2 = S_3$
10:    become(notifying), go around the ring, and then terminate
11: Else wait n units
12: If, while waiting, a notifying agent arrived, terminate.
    /* Rendezvous has occurred. */
13: Else, after waiting, set $r = r + 1$ and repeat from step 3.

One can show the following lemma holds:

Lemma 5.4 (53)   *When an agent sees the same string for the third time, all the other agents have seen it at least twice (in the previous and in the current round).*

Theorem 5.5 (53).   *When the agents have $O(k \log n)$ memory, know n, $\gcd(k', n) = 1$ holds for all $k' \leq k$, $f \leq (k - 1)$ tokens fail, and tokens can fail upon release or later, then the mobile agent rendezvous problem can be solved in $O(kn)$ time.*

Proof. By lemma 5.4, we know that when an agent sees the same string for the third time the meeting point was the true rendezvous point. All the agents met at that point, and after n time units, everybody will terminate. In each round, every agent has spent n time units to compute the inter-token distances, n additional time units to move to the meeting point and wait for the restart, n time units for the termination check. Thus, all agents are perfectly synchronized and start each round, simultaneously. After, at most $k + 2$ rounds rendezvous is accomplished and the total time is then $O(kn)$. $\square$

k KNOWN n UNKNOWN

Lack of knowledge of n makes the situation more complicated; the main problem is to achieve synchronization.

In the following algorithm, if more than one but fewer than k agents meet on a given node, they *merge* and act as one agent for the remainder of the algorithm. Merged agents will be perceived by other agents with their multiplicity; thus, if an agent meets a group of merged agents, it will "see" how many they are. In this algorithm, before starting the next round, every group that has met in a false meeting point, merge and behave like one agent.

Since the agents, not knowing n, cannot travel around the ring, they will travel trying to guess the ring size at each round. Initially, they compute k inter-token distances, and they guess n to be the sum of those distances (they use this guessed value for synchronization purposes); at each subsequent round, they compute one less inter-token distance, and they change their guess of n. The algorithm is designed in such a way that:

1. it is guaranteed that agents are always in at most one round apart,

2. after at most $k - 1$ rounds rendezvous is accomplished.

The pseudocode MEET4 is described in Algorithm 23.

Algorithm 23 (MEET4)

1: Release token.
2: Set $r = 0$, where r denotes a round of the algorithm.
3: Choose a direction and begin walking.
4: Upon meeting another agent, merge with it.
5: Calculate the first $k - r$ inter-token distances, i.e., $S = (d_1, \ldots, d_{k-r})$.
6: Estimate n as $\hat{n} = \sum_{i=1}^{k-r} d_i$.
7: If S is periodic, wait $2\hat{n}$ steps, set $r = r + 1$, and repeat from step 3.
8: Calculate S_{LMR}, the lexicographically maximum rotation of S.
9: Set $t = 0$.
10: Walk to the node that starts S_{LMR} and increment t for each node traveled.
11: Wait $2\hat{n}$ - t clock ticks.
12: If there are k agents or their merged equivalent on the current node, stop.
    /* Rendezvous has occurred. */
13: Else if there are $1 < v < k$ agents on the current node, then merge.
14: Set $r = r + 1$ and repeat from step 3.

The following three lemmata are used in the proof of Theorem 5.9. Their proofs can be found in (53). Lemma 5.6 proves that the agents are always less than a round apart, and thus an agent need only wait $\frac{3\hat{n}}{2}$ clock ticks for any agents that saw the same view.

Lemma 5.6   *Let a be the first agent to finish estimating n in round r, where $0 \leq r \leq k - 1$, and let τ denote the time at which agent a finishes the estimation. All other agents will either finish round $r - 1$ or merge with a on or before time τ.*

Lemma 5.7   *Mobile agents that see the same sequence S, up to a rotation, of inter-token distances are in the same round. If S is aperiodic, then these agents will rendezvous at the end of the given round. However, if S is periodic, then the agents cannot rendezvous during this round and must proceed to the next round.*

Lemma 5.8   *If at most f tokens have failed, then the agents will not execute round $r = f + 1$ in Algorithm MEET4.*

Theorem 5.9   (53).   *When the agents have $O(k \log n)$ memory, know k $\gcd(k', n) = 1$ holds for all $k' \leq k$, $f \leq (k - 1)$ tokens fail, and tokens can fail upon release or later, then the mobile agent rendezvous problem can be solved in $O(k^2 n)$ time.*

Proof. Let $f \leq k - 1$ be the number of tokens that actually fail. Lemma 5.8 implies that no agent will execute more than $f + 1$ rounds of Algorithm MEET4. Suppose that rendezvous has not occurred by the end of round $r = f$. Let a^* denote the first agent that begins round $r = f + 1$ and let t_0 denote the time that a^* starts round $r = f + 1$. Since f tokens have failed, a^*'s estimate for n in round $r = f + 1$ will be correct, i.e., $\hat{n} = n$. The remaining agents see the same aperiodic sequence, up to a rotation, of inter-token distances as a^*, and thus Lemma 5.7 implies that rendezvous occurs at the end of round f.

The number of tokens f that fail, is at most $k - 1$ so, as mentioned above, at most k rounds of Algorithm MEET4 are executed. A round takes at most $k(n - 1)$ time, i.e., the product of the number of inter-token distances measured and the maximum inter-token distance possible. As a result, the time required is $O(k^2 n)$. Because at most k inter-token distances are calculated and the maximum inter-token distance is $n - 1$, the memory required is $O(k \log n)$.   □

5.3.3   THE COST OF TOKEN FAILURE

When tokens fail, the time and memory requirements of the mobile agent rendezvous problem increase. In Table 5.1, we compare the memory and time requirements for rendezvous with and without token failure.

Table 5.1: The Cost of token failure.				
Tokens Fail	Knowledge	Time	Memory	Algorithm
Never	n or k	$O(n)$	$O(\log n)$	Algorithm 11
		$O(n \log k)$	$O(\log k)$	Algorithm 13
Upon release	n	$O(n)$	$O(k \log n)$	MEET1
	k	$O(kn)$	$O(k \log n)$	MEET2
Anytime	n	$O(kn)$	$O(k \log n)$	MEET3
	k	$O(k^2 n)$	$O(k \log n)$	MEET4

5.4   FLICKERING TOKENS

In this section, we introduce a new type of token: the *flickering token*. A *flickering token* is a *probabilistically visible* token occupying a node of the ring. When a mobile agent traverses the node occupied by such a token, it will see the token with probability p, and it will not see the token with probability $1 - p$. We consider trade-offs between memory, time, and number of random bits for flickering tokens.

We will use the term *p-token* when we want to specify the probability associated with the flickering token. We call *token-nodes* the nodes of the ring where the tokens lie, i.e., the initial positions of the agents. We consider two mobile agents in a synchronous, oriented ring. Each of them has a stationary *flickering token*, which it releases at its starting position. When an agent A (respectively, B) is traversing the node occupied by a token, it will see the token with probability p and will not see the token with probability $1 - p$. (See Figure 5.2). For simplicity in the analysis, in this section, we will assume that the agents are an even distance apart on an even size ring.

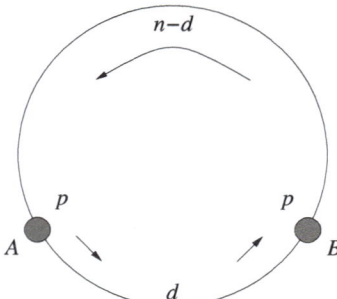

Figure 5.2: Two mobile agents at distance d ($d < n - d$) in an oriented ring with n nodes. Depicted are the short arc (length d) and the long arc (length $n - d$).

Flickering tokens allow two constant memory agents to rendezvous in linear expected time using Algorithm 24. We are interested in computing the expected number of steps of Algorithm 24

Algorithm 24 (Double Token Algorithm: DTA)

1: Leave token at starting position;
2: Repeat until rendezvous;
3: Choose a direction and walk on the nodes of the ring;
4: **If** you see token **then** change direction;
5: **else** stay in same direction.

---

until the mobile agents rendezvous. Our main theorem is the following.

Theorem 5.10 (61). *The expected time until rendezvous for Algorithm 24 is at most*

$$\frac{n}{4p(1-p)} + \frac{n}{4} \quad \text{if the initial MA distance is } d = n/2,$$
$$\frac{1+p(1-p)}{p(1-p)}(n-d) \quad \text{if the initial MA distance is } d < n/2.$$

Also it is $\Theta(n)$.

Before giving the proof of the theorem, we consider two cases, depending on whether or not $d < n/2$.

Case 1: Two MAs at distance $d = n/2$ For the case that n is even and the MAs are at distance $n/2$, we can prove the following lemma.

Lemma 5.11   *Assume n is even and the mobile agents are at distance $d = n/2$. Algorithm 24 is a constant memory algorithm. Moreover, the expected number of steps until the two mobile agents rendezvous is $\frac{n}{4p(1-p)} + \frac{n}{4}$.*

Proof. Initially, the two MAs move in the same direction. It is clear that the two MAs will rendezvous the first time a MA sees the token and the other one will not (This is because the MA that sees the token will change direction.) The probability of this last event is equal to $2p(1-p)$. Since this is a geometric distribution with $2p(1-p)$ the probability of success, it follows that the expected number of rounds until rendezvous will be equal to $\frac{1}{2p(1-p)}$. □

Case 2: Two MAs at distance $d < n/2$ Algorithm 24 can be modeled, of course, as a Markov chain, and its running time is a hitting time (distance between the agents becomes zero for the first time). The difficulty with this particular computation of an expected hitting time is how to describe the states of the Markov chain in a way that takes advantage of the inherent symmetry of the problem. Failing to properly capitalize on this symmetry leads to complicated situations. Also, not every configuration of the agents on the ring will correspond to a state. Only configurations where at least one agent sits on a token-node correspond to states. In a sense, the states correspond to configurations where a direction-reversal may take place. Symmetric or similar configurations of the agents on the ring will correspond to the same state. E.g., we say that the configuration is in an imminent rendezvous state, symbolically an IR-state, if the agents are moving one towards the other with no token-node strictly between them, and at least one agent is at a token-node. The state IR is considered as an absorbing barrier state. Between two consecutive states, i.e., between two consecutive possible direction-reversals, the agent sitting on a token-node as well as the occupied token-node may change. The state will be oblivious to which agent is occupying which token-node. It is also oblivious of the particular node where the agent (not on a token-node) is sitting. It is only the relative positioning between the agents and their relative direction of movement that characterize the states. The direction of movement of an agent on a token-node is considered to be the one after the determination of whether the agent sees the flickering token. Obviously, all nodes apart from the token-nodes belong either to the arc of length d (the shorter one) or to the arc of length $n - d$ (the longer one). We say that an agent is moving inside the shorter arc if it is either at a node of the shorter arc, or is at a token-node and at its next step will be at a node of the shorter arc (or in case $d = 1$, at its next step will be on the other token-node). Similarly for the longer arc.

We introduce three states: $SASD$, $DASD$ and $DADD$ for configurations not in IR and with at least one agent at a token-node. State $SASD$ is characterized by two agents moving inside the same arc at the same direction, irrespectively of whether this is the counterclockwise or clockwise direction. $DASD$ is characterized by two agents moving in different arcs at the same direction, again irrespective of whether this is the counterclockwise or clockwise direction. Finally, $DADD$ is characterized by two agents moving in different arcs at opposing directions.

Between two consecutive states, the agents move for a number of steps, all of which together constitute a single *hyper-step*. A hyper-step is also the collection of steps from an IR-state until rendezvous. The number of steps in a hyper-step is at most $n - d$. To avoid certain degenerate cases, we assume that a state where both agents are at a token-node (either the same or different ones) is nominally *two* consecutive *pseudo-states*, each of exactly one agent on a token-node and with a separating hyper-step of length zero (or, alternatively, of a separating infinitesimally short hyper-step). We assume that these two pseudo-states take place in any order. In other words, one agent arrives at its token-node infinitesimally before the other, and the other infinitesimally after the first has left. There is one hyper-step in between, but it contains zero number of steps. Notice that the introduction of pseudo-states may lead to failed rendezvous even if the agents actually (but not nominally) are concurrently on the same node. For example, when the agents arrive concurrently to the same token-node from opposing directions, and both see the token, then the introduction of pseudo-states forces us not to consider this event as a rendezvous (on the other hand, a rendezvous will take place even under the assumption of pseudo-states if the agents actually, but not nominally, arrive concurrently to the same node from opposing directions and the agent that arrives nominally first misses the flickering token; in this case, the nominally second state will be a barrier IR-state). As this assumption is made only in computing the upper bound for the rendezvous time, it does not affect the correctness of our results. The advantage of the introduction of pseudo-states is that at every state there is unique agent that just arrived on a token-node and, therefore, may have just changed its direction. From now on, we call simply *states* the pseudo-states as well.

Lemma 5.12   *The next state of an $SASD$-state is an IR-state with probability p and a $DASD$-state with probability $1 - p$. The next state of a $DASD$-state is a $DADD$-state with probability p and an $SASD$-state with probability $1 - p$. Finally, the next state of a $DADD$-state is a $DASD$-state with probability p and an IR state with probability $1 - p$.*

Proof. Let X be any state except IR and let X^+ be the next one. Then according to the preceding discussion, at X^+ there is a unique agent arriving at a token-node. If this agent sees the token, then this agent only will change direction of motion, but both agents will remain on their initial arcs. If this agent misses the token, then this agent only will change arc but both agents will retain the direction of their movement.   □

Now, we can complete the proof of the main theorem.

Proof. (Theorem 5.10) Let now $\mathbf{E}_h(X)$ be the expected number of *hyper-steps* until rendezvous when the initial configuration is at state X. Then from the above lemma, we immediately get that:

$$
\begin{aligned}
\mathbf{E}_h(IR) &= 1, & (5.3)\\
\mathbf{E}_h(SASD) &= p\mathbf{E}_h(IR) + (1 - p)\mathbf{E}_h(DASD) + 1, & (5.4)\\
\mathbf{E}_h(DASD) &= p\mathbf{E}_h(DADD) + (1 - p)\mathbf{E}_h(SASD) + 1, & (5.5)\\
\mathbf{E}_h(DADD) &= p\mathbf{E}_h(DASD) + (1 - p)\mathbf{E}_h(IR) + 1. & (5.6)
\end{aligned}
$$

Substituting Equations (5.4) and (5.6) in Equation (5.5) and then making use of Equation (5.3) and finally solving the resulting equation for $\mathbf{E}_h(DASD)$ we get that:

$$
\mathbf{E}_h(DASD) = \frac{1 + p(1 - p)}{p(1 - p)}. \tag{5.7}
$$

If $d = n/2$ then the theorem follows from Lemma 5.11. If $d < n/2$ then we use the previous Markov chain model. Indeed, notice that the initial state of Algorithm 24 is a $DASD$-state, and then use Equation (5.7) taking into account that a hyper-step may have at most $n - d$ steps. For the second statement of the theorem, just observe that there is always a positive probability that the agents move for n steps until rendezvous.   □

5.5   ASYNCHRONOUS RENDEZVOUS

An interesting paper (31) studies the asynchronous version of the rendezvous problem for two agents in arbitrary graphs. Rather than using tokens to break symmetry, it is assumed that each agent has a unique label L which is a nonempty binary string. They assume that each agent knows its own label but not the label of the other agent (though they do know they are different). L_{min} denotes the shorter label and L_{max} the longer one, with ties broken arbitrarily. The agents are initially placed at a distance D from each other. In general, D is not known to the agents. In this setting, it can be shown that meeting at a node is in general impossible, and therefore rendezvous of the agents is allowed inside an edge as well. The measure of performance of a rendezvous algorithm for a given initial location of agents in a graph is the number of edge traversals of both agents until rendezvous is achieved. The network is modeled as an undirected, connected graph. To prevent edge crossings one considers an embedding of the underlying graph in the three-dimensional Euclidean space, with nodes of the graph being points of the space and edges being pairwise disjoint line segments joining them. (Such an embedding exists for any graph.) Mobile agents are modeled as points moving inside this embedding.

Consider networks having an asymmetry, say a distinguished node. Depending on memory capabilities and knowledge of the mobile agents, the rendezvous problem is easy even in the asynchronous case since they can simply be instructed to meet at such a distinguished node. However, this is not the case for networks without asymmetries, and the rendezvous problem in asynchronous settings is non-trivial even for a ring topology.

In fact, we can prove the following theorem.

Theorem 5.13   (31).   *There is an algorithm with cost $O(n|L_{max}|)$ which solves the rendezvous problem for two agents with distinct labels in an n-node asynchronous, unoriented ring. Moreover, if the size n of the ring is known to the agents, then this algorithm can be modified to have cost $O(n|L_{min}|)$, which is optimal.*

The algorithm suggested in the previous theorem and presented in (31) first transforms the label of each agent (by adding binary digits) and then instructs each agent to "execute" its transformed label in order to move.

Consider now the following scenario. The two agents are initially placed at a distance D in an arbitrary asynchronous graph. A map of the graph with labeled ports and indicated initial positions of agents is available to each of them. Having in mind the case of rendezvous in the asynchronous ring, the case of an arbitrary graph can be handled as follows.

Each agent computes the distance D and finds the lexicographically smallest path of length D from its own position to the position of the other agent; both agents can identify the same cycle (which need not be simple, some edges may be repeated, it may even degenerate to one path considered in both directions) of length $2D$ on which their initial positions are situated. Therefore, the solution for the ring can be applied in the general setting of an arbitrary graph.

Theorem 5.14   (31).   *For arbitrary asynchronous graphs, rendezvous of two agents with distinct labels is feasible if an upper bound on the size of the graph is known; moreover, an optimal algorithm of cost $O(D|L_{min}|)$ can be given if a map of the graph and the initial positions of the agents are known to both of them.*

For additional details on the proof, the reader is advised to consult the original paper (31) mentioned above.

5.6   LOOK-COMPUTE-MOVE

5.6.1   MODEL AND TERMINOLOGY

Another interesting investigated setting is the following. Consider an unoriented, anonymous and asynchronous ring. Initially, some nodes of the ring are occupied by robots and there is at most one robot in each node. The goal is to gather all robots in one node of the ring and stop. Robots operate in Look-Compute-Move cycles. In one cycle, a robot takes a snapshot of the current configuration (Look), then, based on the perceived configuration, makes a decision to stay idle or to move to one of its adjacent nodes (Compute), and, in the latter case, makes an instantaneous move to this neighbor (Move). Cycles are performed asynchronously for each robot. This means that the time between Look, Compute, and Move operations is finite but unbounded, and it is decided by the adversary for each robot. The only constraint is that moves are instantaneous, and hence any robot performing a Look operation sees all other robots at nodes of the ring and not on edges, while performing a move. However, a robot R may perform a Look operation at some time t, perceiving robots at some nodes, then Compute a target neighbor at some time $t' > t$, and Move to this neighbor at some later time $t'' > t'$ in which some robots are in different nodes from those previously perceived by R because in the meantime they performed their Move operations. Hence robots may move based on significantly outdated perceptions, which adds to the difficulty of achieving the goal of gathering. It should be stressed that robots are memoryless (oblivious), i.e., they do not have any memory of past observations. Thus the target node (which is either the current position of the robot or one of its neighbors) is decided by the robot during a Compute operation solely on the basis of the location of other robots perceived in the previous Look operation. Robots are anonymous and execute the same deterministic algorithm. They cannot leave any marks at visited nodes nor send any messages to other robots.

An important and well studied capability in the literature on robot gathering is *multiplicity detection* (56; 83). This is the ability of the robots to perceive, during the Look operation, if there is one or more robots in a given location. In our case, we prove that without this capability, gathering of more than one robot is always impossible. Thus we assume the capability of multiplicity detection in our further considerations. It should be stressed that, during a Look operation, a robot can only tell if at some node there are no robots, there is one robot, or there are more than one robots: a robot does not see a difference between a node occupied by a or b robots, for distinct $a, b > 1$.

During the gathering process robots move, and at any time they occupy some nodes of the ring, forming a *configuration*. A configuration is denoted by a pair of sequences $((a_1, \ldots, a_r), (b_1, \ldots, b_s))$, where the integers a_i and b_j have the following meaning. Choose an arbitrary node occupied by at least one robot as node u_1 and consider consecutive nodes $u_1, u_2, u_3, \ldots, u_r$, occupied by at least one robot, starting from u_1 in the clockwise direction. (Clockwise direction is introduced only for the purpose of definition, robots do not have this notion, as the ring is not oriented.) Integer a_i,

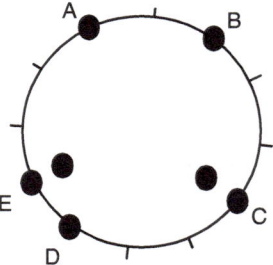

Figure 5.3: A configuration with two multiplicities. The pair of sequences describing this configuration starting from robot A is $((2, 3, 3, 1, 3), (5, 9))$. The view of robot A is $\{((2, 3, 3, 1, 3), (5, 9)), ((3, 1, 3, 3, 2), (3, 7))\}$.

for $i < r$, denotes the distance in the ring between nodes u_i and u_{i+1}, and integer a_r denotes the distance between nodes u_r and u_1 (in the clockwise direction). Next, consider those nodes among $u_1, u_2, u_3, \ldots, u_r$ which are occupied by more than one robot. Such nodes are called *multiplicities*. Suppose that $u_{v_1}, \ldots, u_{v_s}$ are these consecutive nodes (ordered in clockwise direction). Integer b_i is defined as the distance in the clockwise direction between node u_1 and node u_{v_i}. It should be clear that different choices of node u_1 give rise to different pairs of sequences. Respective sequences in these pairs are cyclic shifts of each other and correspond to the same positioning of robots. For configurations without multiplicities, we will drop the second sequence, simply using sequence $(a_1, \ldots, a_r)$. An example of a configuration with two multiplicities is shown in Figure 5.3.

Consider a configuration $C = (a_1, \ldots, a_r)$ without multiplicities. We call *range* of the configuration C the set $\{a_1, \ldots, a_r\}$. For any integer a_i in the range of C, we call *weight* of a_i the number of times this integer appears in the sequence $(a_1, \ldots, a_r)$. C is called *periodic* if the sequence $(a_1, \ldots, a_r)$ is a concatenation of at least two copies of a subsequence p. A periodic configuration is shown in Figure 5.4. The configuration C can be also represented as the set Z of nodes occupied by the robots. C is called *symmetric* if there exists an axis of symmetry of the ring, such that the set Z is symmetric with respect to this axis. If the number of robots is odd and S is an axis of symmetry of the set Z, then there is exactly one robot on the axis S. This robot is called *axial* for this axis. A symmetric configuration is shown in Figure 5.5. Notice that all cases are possible for a configuration: symmetric, periodic, both symmetric and periodic, neither symmetric nor periodic. A configuration, which is periodic and symmetric, is shown in Figure 5.6. Two robots are called *neighboring*, if at least one of the two segments of the ring between them does not contain any robots. A segment of the ring between two neighboring robots is called *free* if there is no robot in this segment.

We now describe formally what a robot perceives during a Look operation. Fix a robot R in a configuration represented by a pair of sequences $((a_1, \ldots, a_r), (b_1, \ldots, b_s))$, where this particular representation is taken with respect to the node occupied by R (i.e., this node is con-

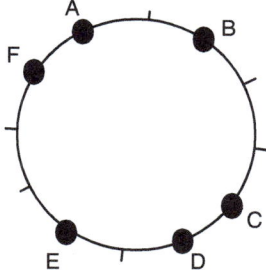

Figure 5.4: A periodic configuration. The sequence describing this configuration starting from robot A is $(2, 3, 1, 2, 3, 1)$. The view of robots A and D is $\{(2, 3, 1, 2, 3, 1), (1, 3, 2, 1, 3, 2)\}$. Robots B and E have the same view $\{(3, 1, 2, 3, 1, 2), (2, 1, 3, 2, 1, 3)\}$. Robots C and F have the same view $\{(1, 2, 3, 1, 2, 3), (3, 2, 1, 3, 2, 1)\}$.

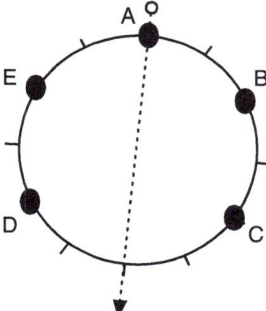

Figure 5.5: A symmetric configuration. The sequence describing this configuration starting from robot A is $(2, 2, 4, 2, 2)$. The view of robot A is $\{(2, 2, 4, 2, 2), (2, 2, 4, 2, 2)\}$. Robots B and E have the same view $\{(2, 4, 2, 2, 2), (2, 2, 2, 4, 2)\}$. Robots C and D have the same view $\{(4, 2, 2, 2, 2), (2, 2, 2, 2, 4)\}$.

sidered as node u_1). The *view* of robot R is the set of two pairs of sequences $\{((a_1, \ldots, a_r),$ $(b_1, \ldots, b_s)), ((a_r, a_{r-1}, \ldots, a_1), (n - b_s, \ldots, n - b_1))\}$ (if the node occupied by R is a multiplicity then we define the view of R as $\{((a_1, \ldots, a_r), (0, b_2, \ldots, b_s)), ((a_r, a_{r-1}, \ldots, a_1), (0, n - b_s, \ldots, n - b_2))\}$). This formalization captures the fact that the ring is unoriented and hence the robot R cannot distinguish between a configuration and its symmetric image, if R is itself on the axis of symmetry. This is conveyed by defining the view as the *set* of the two couple of sequences because the sets

$$\{((a_1, \ldots, a_r), (b_1, \ldots, b_s)), ((a_r, a_{r-1}, \ldots, a_1), (n - b_s, \ldots, n - b_1))\}$$

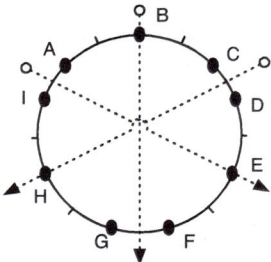

Figure 5.6: A symmetric and periodic configuration. The sequence describing this configuration starting from robot A is $(2, 2, 1, 2, 2, 1, 2, 2, 1)$. This configuration has 3 axes of symmetry. The view of robots A, C, D, F, G, I is $\{(2, 2, 1, 2, 2, 1, 2, 2, 1), (1, 2, 2, 1, 2, 2, 1, 2, 2)\}$. The view of robots B, E, H is $\{(2, 1, 2, 2, 1, 2, 2, 1, 2), (2, 1, 2, 2, 1, 2, 2, 1, 2)\}$.

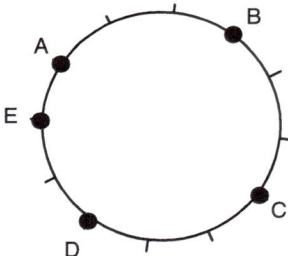

Figure 5.7: A rigid configuration. The views of robots A, B, C, D, E are $\{(3, 3, 3, 2, 1), (1, 2, 3, 3, 3)\}$, $\{(3, 3, 2, 1, 3), (3, 1, 2, 3, 3)\}$, $\{(3, 2, 1, 3, 3), (3, 3, 1, 2, 3)\}$, $\{(2, 1, 3, 3, 3), (3, 3, 3, 1, 2)\}$ and $\{(1, 3, 3, 3, 2), (2, 3, 3, 3, 1)\}$, respectively.

and

$$\{((a_r, a_{r-1}, \ldots, a_1), (n - b_s, \ldots, n - b_1)), ((a_1, \ldots, a_r), (b_1, \ldots, b_s))\}$$

are equal. As before, if there are no multiplicities, we will drop the second sequence in each case and write the view as the set of two sequences: $\{(a_1, \ldots, a_r), (a_r, a_{r-1}, \ldots, a_1)\}$. For example, in a 9-node ring with consecutive nodes $1, \ldots, 9$ and three robots occupying nodes 1,2,4, the view of robot R at node 1 is the set $\{(1, 2, 6), (6, 2, 1)\}$.

A configuration without multiplicities is called *rigid* if the views of all robots are distinct. A rigid configuration is shown in Figure 5.7. We can show the following lemma:

Lemma 5.15

1. *A configuration without multiplicities is non-rigid, if and only if it is either periodic or symmetric.*

2. *If a configuration without multiplicities is non-rigid and non-periodic, then it has exactly one axis of symmetry.*

Consider a configuration without multiplicities that is non-rigid and non-periodic. Then it is symmetric. Let S be its unique axis of symmetry. If the number of robots is odd, then exactly one robot is situated on S and S goes through the antipodal node if the size n of the ring is even, and through the (middle of the) antipodal edge if n is odd. If the number of robots is even, then two cases are possible:

- *edge-edge symmetry*: S goes through (the middles of) two antipodal edges;

- *node-on-axis symmetry*: at least one node is on the axis of symmetry.

Note, that the first case can occur only for an even number of robots in a ring of even size.

5.6.2 IMPOSSIBILITY RESULTS

Lemma 5.16

1. *Gathering any 2 robots is impossible on any ring.*

2. *If multiplicity detection is not available, then gathering any $k > 1$ robots is impossible on any ring.*

Proof. To prove the first part, consider a gathering algorithm for 2 robots. In any configuration, the robots have the same view. Consider what the algorithm does if the distance between the robots is 1. If the algorithm tells the robots not to move, then it is clearly incorrect. If it tells them to move then a synchronous adversary that schedules all operations of both robots simultaneously does not permit gathering: the robots will always be at odd distance (in the case when the algorithm tells them to move towards each other when at distance 1, this adversary forces perpetual swapping).

The proof of the second part is by induction on k. For $k = 2$, it follows from part 1. Suppose that the statement is true for all numbers $k' < k$ of robots and consider a gathering algorithm for k robots. Consider the configuration C just before the first multiplicity is created. Then, at least one robot R moves to an adjacent node occupied by another robot. Consider an adversary that first schedules a Look and a Move operation only for robot R, and only then schedules the next Look operations for other robots. Robot R will create a multiplicity, thus reducing the number of nodes occupied by robots to $k - 1$. All subsequent Look operations will be performed for at most $k - 1$ nodes occupied by robots. Since multiplicity detection is not available, the perceptions of the robots will be the same as in the case of less than k robots. By the inductive hypothesis, gathering is thus impossible. □

Lemma 5.16 justifies the two assumptions made throughout this section: the number k of robots is at least 3 and robots are capable of multiplicity detection.

Theorem 5.17 (63).   *Gathering is impossible for any periodic configuration.*

Proof. Consider a periodic configuration with the period repeated $t > 1$ times. Consider an adversary synchronously scheduling all operations in rounds: first, the Look operation for all robots, then the Compute operation for all robots, then the Move operation for all robots, and so on. We remind the reader that the robots are oblivious, i.e., they do not have any memory of past observations. The configuration is periodic in round 0. Suppose it is periodic in round r. The views of all t corresponding robots in the t copies of the period are identical in round r and hence the configuration remains periodic in round $r + 1$, with t copies of the period. By induction, the configuration remains periodic in every round, with t copies of the period. Since $t > 1$, gathering will never occur.   □

The following impossibility result concerns only the case of an even number of robots on a ring of even size.

Theorem 5.18 (63).   *Gathering is impossible for any edge-edge symmetric configuration.*

Proof. Consider a configuration which has an edge-edge symmetry. This means that both the size of the ring and the number of robots are even. Consider an adversary synchronously scheduling all operations in rounds: first the Look operation for all robots, then the Compute operation for all robots, then the Move operation for all robots, and so on. The configuration is symmetric in round 0. Suppose it is symmetric in round r. If robot R' is the symmetric image of robot R with respect to this symmetry then the distance between R and R' is odd. Robots R and R' have identical views in round r, hence they will behave identically (robots are oblivious), and their distance in round $r + 1$ will change either by 0, or by 2 or by -2. This implies that in round $r + 1$ the configuration will remain symmetric (robots R and R' have again the same view), and the distance between robots R and R' will remain odd. By induction, the configuration remains symmetric, and the distance between a robot and its symmetric image remains odd, in all rounds. This implies that gathering will never occur.   □

5.6.3   GATHERING CONFIGURATIONS WITH A SINGLE MULTIPLICITY

We now show a gathering procedure for any configuration containing exactly one multiplicity, say at node v. The idea is to gather all robots at v, avoiding creating another multiplicity (which could potentially create a symmetry, making the gathering process harder or even impossible). The following procedure achieves this goal by first moving the robots closest to v towards v, then moving there the second closest robots, and so on. The correctness of Procedure `Single-Multiplicity-Gathering` is straightforward.

Procedure Single-Multiplicity-Gathering

1: **if** R is at the multiplicity **then**

2:   do not move

3: **else**

4:   **if** none of the segments between R and the multiplicity is free **then**

5:     do not move

6:   **else**

7:     move towards the multiplicity along the shortest of the free segments or along any of them in the case of equality

8:   **end if**

9: **end if**

5.6.4   GATHERING RIGID CONFIGURATIONS

Let us now discuss a gathering procedure for any rigid configuration, regardless of the number of robots. The main idea of the procedure is to elect a single robot and move it until it hits one of its neighboring robots, thus creating a single multiplicity, and then to apply Procedure `Single-Multiplicity-Gathering`. The elected robot must be such that during its walk the rigidity property is not lost. In order to achieve this goal, we perform the election as follows. First, the robots elect a pair of neighboring robots at maximum distance (there may be several such pairs, whence the need for election). Then they choose among them the robot, which has the other neighboring robot closer. Ties can be broken easily (see the details of the algorithm).

In order to elect a robot, we need to linearly order all possible views. This can be done in many ways. One of them is to order lexicographically all finite sequences of integers and number them by consecutive natural numbers. Then a view becomes a set of two natural numbers. Treat these sets as ordered pairs of natural numbers in increasing order, order these pairs lexicographically, and assign them consecutive natural numbers in increasing order. We fix the resulting linear order of views and this numbering beforehand, adding it to the algorithm for all robots. The natural number assigned to a view will be called the *code* of this view.

Lemma 5.19   *Procedure Rigid-Gathering performs gathering of robots for any rigid configuration without multiplicities.*

Proof. Suppose that robots M and N at distance Max are elected in the first part of the procedure. Suppose, without loss of generality, that the distance a between M and M' is less than the distance b between N and N'. Then robot M moves towards M_2. After this move, the distance between M and N becomes $Max + 1$, and the distance between M and M_2 becomes $a - 1$. No other distances between neighboring robots change. Hence in the new configuration, M and N are again neighboring robots at maximum distance. The configuration is again rigid because M and N are the unique pair of neighboring robots at distance $Max + 1$ and the distance $a - 1$ between M and M_2 is smaller

---

Procedure Rigid-Gathering

1: $Max \leftarrow$ the largest of the distances a_i in the view of R

2: $M \leftarrow$ robot with largest code of view having a neighboring robot at distance Max

3: $N \leftarrow$ robot with largest code of view having M as a neighboring robot at distance Max /* the pair of robots at distance Max is elected. */

4: $j \leftarrow 1$; $M_1 \leftarrow M$; $N_1 \leftarrow N$; $M_0 \leftarrow N$; $N_0 \leftarrow M$;

5: **repeat**

6:    $j \leftarrow j + 1$;

7:    $M_j \leftarrow$ the neighboring robot of M_{j-1} different from M_{j-2}

8:    $N_j \leftarrow$ the neighboring robot of N_{j-1} different from N_{j-2}

9: **until** the distance between N and N_j is different than the one between M and M_j

10: $N' \leftarrow N_j$; $M' \leftarrow M_j$;

11: **if** there is no multiplicity **then**

12:    **if** distance between N and N' is smaller than the one between M and M' **then**

13:       **if** $R = N$ **then**

14:          move towards N_2

15:       **end if**

16:    **else**

17:       **if** $R = M$ **then**

18:          move towards M_2

19:       **end if**

20:    **end if**

21: **else**

22:    Single-Multiplicity-Gathering

23: **end if**

---

than the distance b between N and N_2. Robots M and N are again elected because now there is only one neighboring pair of robots at the maximum distance $Max + 1$. Since the distance $a - 1$ between M and M_2 is smaller than the distance b between N and N_2, it is again the robot M that will move towards M_2. It follows that, until a multiplicity is created, only one robot will move, and it will move in the same direction. This guarantees that a multiplicity will be finally created, and it will be unique. Hence Procedure `Single-Multiplicity-Gathering` will be applied, thus completing gathering.   □

5.6.5   GATHERING AN ODD NUMBER OF ROBOTS

We finally present a gathering algorithm (Algorithm 25) for any non-periodic configuration of an odd number of robots. Together with Theorem 5.17, this algorithm solves the gathering problem for an odd number of robots. The idea of the algorithm is the following. Consider any non-periodic configuration of an odd number of robots (recall that initially there are no multiplicities). If it is rigid, then apply Procedure `Rigid-Gathering`. Otherwise, it must be symmetric, by Lemma 5.15. There is a unique axial robot for its unique axis of symmetry. Move this robot to any adjacent node. We prove below that three cases can occur.

(1) The resulting situation has a multiplicity (the adjacent node was occupied by a robot): then apply Procedure `Single-Multiplicity-Gathering`.

(2) The resulting configuration is rigid: then apply Procedure `Rigid-Gathering`.

(3) Another axis of symmetry has been created (the previous one has been obviously destroyed by the move). In this case, there is a unique axial robot for the unique axis of symmetry. Move this robot to any adjacent node. Again one of the three above cases can occur.

Nevertheless, we prove that after a finite number of such moves, only cases (1) or (2) can occur, and thus gathering is finally accomplished either by applying Procedure `Single-Multiplicity-Gathering` or by applying Procedure `Rigid-Gathering`.

Algorithm 25 (Odd-Gathering)

1: **if** the configuration is periodic **then**
2:    output: gathering impossible
3: **else**
4:    **if** the configuration has a single multiplicity **then**
5:        Single-Multiplicity-Gathering
6:    **else**
7:        **if** the configuration is rigid **then**
8:            Rigid-Gathering
9:        **else**
10:           **if** R is axial **then**
11:               move (to any of the adjacent nodes)
12:           **end if**
13:        **end if**
14:    **end if**
15: **end if**

Before starting to prove the correctness of Algorithm 25, let us give an example of its execution.

Example 5.20   Consider the configuration $C = (a, a + 1, a - 1, a + 1, a - 1, a + 1, a)$ of 7 robots, for some $a > 1$ (see Figure 5.8(i)). This is a symmetric non-periodic configuration with the axial robot at distance a from its neighboring robots. After moving the axial robot towards one of its neighboring robots, we obtain the configuration $C' = (a + 1, a + 1, a - 1, a + 1, a - 1, a + 1, a - 1)$ as shown in Figure 5.8(ii), which is again symmetric and non-periodic. Its axial robot is at

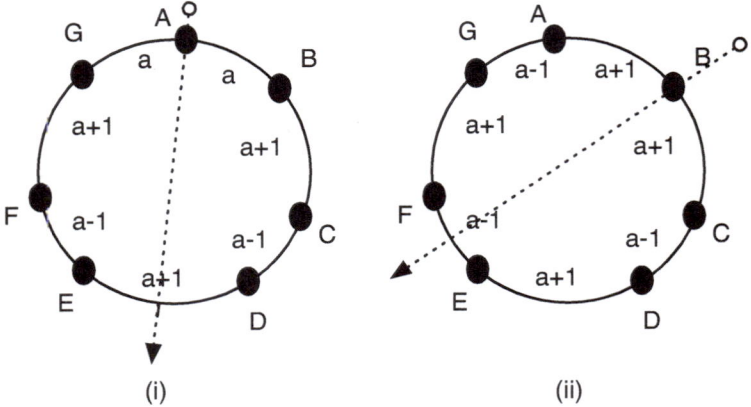

Figure 5.8: A series of non-periodic, symmetric configurations.

distance $a + 1$ from its neighboring robots. After moving the axial robot of C' towards any one of its neighboring robots, we obtain a rigid configuration in which gathering can be completed using Procedure `Rigid-Gathering`.

Lemma 5.21   *Let C be a symmetric configuration of an odd number of robots, without multiplicities. Let C' be the configuration resulting from C by moving the axial robot to any of the adjacent nodes. Assume that C' does not have multiplicities. Then C' is not periodic.*

Proof. Since C is symmetric, C' is of the form $(a + 1, b_1, \ldots, b_{s-1}, b_s, b_{s-1}, \ldots, b_1, a - 1)$. Suppose that C' is periodic and take the period d of a length p in which $d_1 = a + 1$ (the first term of the period d is the first term of C'). Then $d_p = a - 1$ (the last term of the period d is the last term of C'). Since C is symmetric, it must hold that $d_p = d_1$. Contradiction.   □

Theorem 5.22 (63).   *Algorithm 25 performs gathering of any non-periodic configuration of an odd number of robots.*

In order to prove Theorem 5.22, we need the following technical lemmas.

Lemma 5.23   *Let Cf be a symmetric non-periodic configuration of an odd number of robots, without multiplicities. Then exactly one value in the range of Cf has odd weight.*

Proof. By Lemma 5.15, the configuration Cf has exactly one axis of symmetry. Let S be this axis, and let C and D be the unique pair of neighboring robots, situated on the opposite sides of S (see Figure 5.5). Let x be the length of the free segment between C and D. Consider any value y different from x, in the range of Cf. For every pair of neighboring robots with the free segment between them of length y, there is the symmetric pair of robots with the same length of the free segment between them. This implies that y must have even weight. On the other hand, for every pair of neighboring robots different from C, D, with the free segment between them of length x, there is the symmetric pair of robots with the same length of the free segment between them. In view of the existence of the pair C, D, this implies that x must have odd weight. □

Let Cf be a symmetric non-periodic configuration of an odd number of robots, without multiplicities (see Figure 5.5 for an example). The unique value of odd weight in the configuration Cf is called the *chief* of Cf. This is the value of the length of the free segment between the two neighboring robots situated on the opposite sides of the axis of symmetry. The distance between the axial robot and its neighboring robots is called the *index* of Cf. Let Cf$'$ be the configuration resulting from Cf by moving the axial robot to any of the adjacent nodes. If Cf$'$ does not have multiplicities and is symmetric, then we will call it *special*. In Figure 5.5, the chief is the value of the length of the free segment between robots C and D. The index is the value of the distance between robots A and E (or A and B).

Lemma 5.24   *Let C be a symmetric non-periodic configuration of an odd number of robots, without multiplicities. Let z and f be the index and chief of C, respectively. Let C' be the configuration resulting from C by moving the axial robot to any of the adjacent nodes. If C' is special then $z = f - 1$ or $z = f + 1$ and the chief of C' is either $z + 1$ or $z - 1$.*

Proof. If the weights of $z + 1$ and $z - 1$ are both even in C', then both of them must have been odd in C. But this contradicts Lemma 5.23. For the same reason, exactly one of them has an odd weight in C. Therefore, the chief f in C is either $f = z - 1$ or $f = z + 1$. Additionally, exactly one of $z - 1$ and $z + 1$ has an even weight in C and thus an odd weight in C' and that is the chief of C'. □

Consider a special configuration C. We define the following sets:

- *White part*: the set of those integers in the range of C with the same parity as that of the chief.

- *Black part*: the set of those integers in the range of C with different parity than that of the chief.

For example, if the chief of C is an odd number then the white part is the set of odd integers while the black part is the set of even integers in the range of C.

We denote by $b(C)$ the total number of occurrences in C of integers from the black part of its range.

Lemma 5.25   *Consider a special configuration C. Let C' be the configuration resulting from C by moving the axial robot to any of the adjacent nodes. If C' is special then $b(C') < b(C)$.*

Proof. Let z be the index of C, and f its chief. By Lemma 5.24, we have either $z = f - 1$ or $z = f + 1$. Consider the first case, i.e., $f = z + 1$. In the configuration C', the weight of each of the integers $z + 1$ and $z - 1$ increases by 1 and the weight of integer z decreases by 2. Since the weight of f was odd in C, now it becomes even. Since the weight of $z - 1$ was even, now it becomes odd and $z - 1$ is the chief of C'. The parity of the chief does not change with respect to the configuration C. Hence z (if it still has positive weight in C') is in the black part of the range of C' because it has parity different from that of the chief. Integers $z - 1$ and $z + 1$ are in the white part of the range. No other weights change in comparison with C. It follows that the sum of weights in the black part of C' is by 2 smaller than the sum of weights in the black part of C. The argument in the second case, i.e., when $f = z - 1$, is analogous. □

Corollary 5.26   *Consider a sequence $(C_1, C_2, \dots)$ of special configurations, such that C_{i+1} results from C_i by moving the axial robot to any of the adjacent nodes. Then for some $i \le k$, we have $b(C_i) = 0$.*

Lemma 5.27   *Consider a special configuration C, with $b(C) = 0$. Let C' be the configuration resulting from C by moving the axial robot to any of the adjacent nodes. If C' does not have multiplicities then it is not symmetric.*

Proof. If C' were symmetric, then it would be special. This contradicts Lemma 5.25 in view of $b(C) = 0$. □

We are now ready to prove the correctness of Algorithm 25 (Theorem 5.22).

Proof. (Theorem 5.22) Consider an initial non-periodic configuration C of an odd number of robots. By assumption it does not contain multiplicities. If it is rigid, then we are done by Lemma 5.19. Otherwise, it must be symmetric by Lemma 5.15. Let A be its unique axial robot. Let C_1 be the configuration resulting from C by moving robot A to any of the adjacent nodes. If C_1 contains a multiplicity, then we are done by applying Procedure Single-Multiplicity-Gathering. If C_1 is rigid, then we are done by Lemma 5.19. Otherwise, C_1 is either periodic or symmetric, in view of Lemma 5.15. By Lemma 5.21, it cannot be periodic, hence it must be symmetric, and thus special. Consider the configuration C_2 resulting by moving the axial robot of C_1 to any of the adjacent nodes. Again C_2 either contains a multiplicity, or is rigid, or is special. In the first two cases, we are done, and in the third case the axial robot is moved again. In this way, we create a sequence $C_1, C_2, \dots$ of special configurations. By Lemma 5.26, there is a configuration C_i in this sequence, with $b(C_i) = 0$. Let

C' be the configuration resulting from C_i by moving the axial robot to any of the adjacent nodes. By Lemma 5.27, the configuration C' either has a multiplicity, or cannot be symmetric, and thus must be rigid. In the first case, we are done by applying Procedure `Single-Multiplicity-Gathering` and in the second case by Lemma 5.19. □

As a corollary of Theorems 5.22 and 5.17 we obtain:

Corollary 5.28 *For an odd number of robots, gathering is feasible if and only if the initial configuration is not periodic.*

For the remaining case, (i.e., an even number of robots with a node-on-axis symmetry), the authors in (62) provide an algorithm which solves the gathering problem for non-periodic configurations of more than 18 agents. Their approach is based on preserving (rather than breaking) symmetry.

5.7 DANGEROUS NETWORKS

In this section, we consider dangerous networks which contain hostile hosts of a particularly harmful nature, called *black holes*. A black hole is a stationary process residing at a node of a network and destroying all mobile agents visiting the node, without leaving any trace. The only way to locate a black hole is to visit it by at least one agent. The problem of locating a black hole in a network (*Black Hole Search (BHS) problem*), has been investigated in asynchronous and synchronous networks.

In order to understand some basic properties of such dangerous networks, we will first present some results for the BHS problem in asynchronous rings, and then we will discuss the solvability of rendezvous problem in spite of black holes.

5.7.1 BLACK-HOLE SEARCH IN AN ASYNCHRONOUS RING

We study here the BHS problem in an asynchronous ring topology. We first discuss the model and give lower bounds on the number of agents and time-complexity. We then give two algorithms that solve the problem using two or more co-located mobile agents.

MODEL AND LOWER BOUNDS ON THE RING TOPOLOGY

We consider two anonymous co-located agents, i.e., the agents start at the same node h. The ring is anonymous, asynchronous and consists of n nodes. On each node, there is a *whiteboard* where the agents can leave messages. The access on a whiteboard is done using mutual exclusion and hence the agents can acquire distinct identities by the order in which they access the whiteboard (e.g., the first agent accessing the whiteboard creates a counter on it, initializes it to 1 and gets this identity, while the next agent increases the counter and take its value as its identity). Although the ring is anonymous, the distinct identities assigned to agents, allow them to agree on the clockwise direction.

It is easy to see that, if there is only one agent, the BHS problem is unsolvable since the only agent would necessarily vanish into the black hole.

Lemma 5.29   *At least two agents are needed to locate the black hole.*

Due to network asynchrony, it is impossible to distinguish between a "slow" link and a link leading to a black hole. This observation gives us the following two lemmas.

Lemma 5.30   *The problem of whether there exists or not a black hole in an asynchronous network is unsolvable.*

Lemma 5.31   *It is impossible to locate the black hole if the size of the network is unknown.*

Proof. For the sake of contradiction, assume that there is an algorithm A which without knowledge of the size of the network, locates the black hole. Consider a synchronous execution of A on a ring R consisting of the nodes $x_0, x_1, ..., x_{n-1}$, which leads $k \geq 2$ co-located agents to find the black hole after a finite time t. Suppose that the agents are initially situated at x_0 and the black hole is at node x_b. Now consider a ring R' with nodes $x_0, x_1, ..., x_{b-1}, u, z, v, x_{b+1}, ..., x_{n-1}$, where x_0 is the homebase and the black hole is at z. Suppose that the adversary introduces delays in R' exactly as in R except from the links (x_{b-1}, u) and (x_{b+1}, v) where the delays are more than t time units. All agents which moved towards x_b from x_{b-1} or x_{b+1} and were perished in the execution of A in R, will now (in R') move towards u or v, respectively. However, they will not arrive there until after time t. During the first t time units, all the other agents will experience the same situation in R' as in R and hence they will take the same decisions. Therefore, the agents will incorrectly report that the links (x_{b-1}, u) and (x_{b+1}, v) are incident to the black hole. $\square$

Theorem 5.32   (39).   *Any algorithm needs at least $2n - 4$ moves to find the black hole in a ring, regardless of the number of agents available.*

Proof. In order to report the position of the black hole back to node h, the agents need to receive information from any other node apart from the node b containing the black hole. This means that every node apart from b has to be visited by at least one agent. Suppose that the black hole resides at a neighbor node counter-clockwise from h and hence $n - 1$ nodes clockwise from h. Then an agent must travel clockwise to node $n - 2$ and then an agent must report back to h. Therefore, a total number of $2n - 4$ steps must be taken. $\square$

AN ALGORITHM FOR TWO AGENTS SOLVING THE BHS PROBLEM ON A RING

We denote with U and E the unexplored and explored area, respectively. We also denote with U^L and U^R the continuous unexplored area adjacent counter-clockwise and clockwise, respectively, from the explored area. A basic tool which is used in the algorithm is the *Cautious Walk* (introduced in (39)):

Consider an agent situated at a node v_0 adjacent to an unexplored node v_1. The agent explores a previously unexplored area $U_k = < v_1, v_2, \ldots, v_k >$ in the following way:

Cautious Walk:

- before leaving a node v_i going to a node v_{i+1}, the agent marks the port leading from v_i to v_{i+1} as *active*,

- immediately after visiting v_{i+1}, the agent returns to v_i, and marks the port leading from v_i to v_{i+1} as *safe*,

- the agent checks for messages at v_i and (if such a message exists) re-assigns to itself an unexplored area U'_k which has to discover and repeats from the start.

The agents know the size n of the ring. They follow Algorithm 26. A high level description of the algorithm is the following:

Suppose the agents start at node h. Using mutual exclusion they write at the whiteboard of node h and get distinct identities as described in the beginning of the section. Then they divide the unexplored area U with $|U| = n - 1$ into two disjoint paths U^L and U^R with $|U^L| = \lceil \frac{n-1}{2} \rceil$ and $|U^R| = \lfloor \frac{n-1}{2} \rfloor$. Agent 1 explores the area U^L and agent 2 explores the area U^R using *Cautious Walk*. Since there is exactly one black hole, and the two sets are continuous and disjoint, after a finite time exactly one of the agents will finish with the exploration. Suppose without loss of generality that agent 1 finishes. Then agent 1 traverses back through the explored area until it meets a node u whose port leading to a node v has not been marked as safe. At that point, agent 1 updates explored area and divides the updated unexplored area into new continuous and disjoint paths U^L and U^R having U^L starting at a node situated anti-clockwise from h and U^R starting at a node situated clockwise from h. Assigns U^L to itself and U^R to agent 2 and leaves this message at node u. Now agent 1 traverses the explored area and explores its new assigned path U^L. Agent 2 either travels through a slow link (not having explored its assigned area) or vanished in the black-hole. In the first case, agent 2 will first return at node u, will check for messages and update its assigned area for exploration. The agents repeat this procedure until exactly one of them vanishes into the black-hole. Then the other agent which repeats the procedure, will eventually come up with an explored area of size $n - 1$. At that point, it knows the exact location of the black-hole.

Theorem 5.33 (39).   *Algorithm 26 locates the black-hole within $O(n \log n)$ moves.*

Algorithm 26 (BHSRing)

1: Assign distinct identities to agents
2: Divide U into two continuous disjoint parts U^L (starting anti-clockwise of node h) and U^R (starting clockwise of node h) of almost equal sizes
3: Assign U^L to agent 1 and U^R to agent 2 and leave a message at h
4: **while** $|E| < n - 1$ **do**
5:     Agent 1 explores U^L using *Cautious Walk*
6:     Agent 2 explores U^R using *Cautious Walk*
7:     Agent 1(2) traverses clockwise (anti-clockwise) the explored area until it reaches a node u with a not safe port
8:     Update E and U
9:     **if** $|U| > 1$ **then**
10:         Divide U into two continuous disjoint parts U^L and U^R of almost equal sizes, and leave a message at v
11:     **end if**
12: **end while**
13: Report the black-hole location

Proof. Initially, the explored area consists of one node. Since the two agents divide the unexplored area into two disjoint sets, exactly one of the agents will finish the exploration of its assigned set after a finite time and will be called the *traveling* agent. The other agent can not complete the exploration of its part (since it contains the black hole), and will be called *blocked*. Let e_i be the size of the total explored area up to phase ϕ_i (each phase ϕ_i starts with the agent situated at a border node of the explored area E_{i-1} (of phase ϕ_{i-1}) and finishes when the agent passes from the homebase after leaving a message). Let p_i be the number of links traversed by the *blocked* agent of phase ϕ_i. According to Algorithm 26, the size e_i of the explored area during phase ϕ_i is equal to half of the size of the unexplored area of the previous phase, plus the new area explored by the current *blocked* agent. Hence the total area explored at the end of phase ϕ_i is: $e_i \leq \lceil \frac{1}{2}(n - e_{i-1}) \rceil + p_i + e_{i-1} \leq \frac{1}{2}(n + e_{i-1}) + p_i + 1$. The work (total number of moves) w_i done by the traveling agent in each phase is (due to *Cautious Walk*):

$$w_i \leq 4 \left(\left\lceil \frac{n - e_{i-1}}{2} \right\rceil - 1 \right) + 2 + 2e_{i-1} + 2p_i \leq 2n + 2p_i + 2$$

Thus the total work in all $s = \log n$ phases is:

$$\sum_{i=1}^{s} w_i \leq 2 \sum_{i=1}^{s} p_i + 2sn + 2s \leq 2 \left\lceil \frac{n-1}{2} \right\rceil + 2n \log n + 2 \log n$$

Therefore, the total number of moves is $O(n \log n)$.   □

A natural question is the following: Can we decrease the time needed for Black Hole Search if we have $k \geq 2$ available co-located agents?

AN ALGORITHM FOR $n - 1$ AGENTS SOLVING THE BHS PROBLEM ON A RING

Algorithm 27 shows that $n - 1$ co-located agents can locate the black hole in $2n - 4$ moves.

Algorithm 27 (OptTime)

 1: Assign distinct identities to agents
 2: Agent i travels $i - 1$ edges in clockwise direction
 3: Agent i travels $n - 2$ edges in counter-clockwise direction
 4: Agent i returns to homebase traveling in clockwise direction
 5: Agent i reports that the black hole resides at node i

In Algorithm 27, it should be clear that among the $n - 1$ agents, exactly one will finish the algorithm, while all the other $n - 2$ agents will vanish into the black hole.

Theorem 5.34 (39). *Algorithm 27 lets $n - 1$ co-located agents find the black hole in $2n - 4$ moves.*

Proof. Suppose that the black hole resides at a node b which is b steps clockwise from node 0. Then agent with label b travels $b - 1 + n - 2 + n - (b + 1) = 2n - 4$. □

5.7.2 RENDEZVOUS IN ASYNCHRONOUS RINGS IN SPITE OF A BLACK-HOLE

We discuss now how k dispersed agents can rendezvous in an anonymous, asynchronous ring in spite of a black hole. We first give some feasibility results.

Theorem 5.35 (40). *Let k agents be in an anonymous ring with a black hole:*

1. *It is impossible for all k agents to rendezvous.*

2. *If the ring is unoriented, then it is impossible for $k - 1$ agents to rendezvous.*

Proof. To prove part 1, observe that since the location of the black hole is unknown to the agents, the first agent that moves could immediately disappear in the black hole and will never be able to gather.

To prove part 2, observe that since there is no directional agreement, two agents could disappear in the black hole from both sides at their first move and will not be able to gather. □

Theorem 5.36   (40).   *If k is unknown, then rendezvous requires locating the black hole.*

Proof. If the black hole is not located, then there can be unexplored nodes (i.e., nodes whose ports are all unexplored) that can contain agents not participating to the gathering.   □

In view of Lemma 5.31 and Theorem 5.36 the following theorem holds:

Theorem 5.37   (40).   *Either k or n must be known for rendezvous.*

n UNKNOWN, *k* KNOWN, ORIENTED RING

Rendezvous of dispersed agents can be solved easily in the "whiteboard" model in an oriented anonymous, asynchronous ring in spite of a black hole when k is known (see Algorithm 28). In this case, one agent will vanish in the black hole while the rest will rendezvous.

Algorithm 28 (Gathering)

 1: Each agent moves along the ring clockwise using cautious walk
 2: When arriving at a node already visited by another agent, it proceeds clockwise to the next node via the safe port. If there is no safe port, it tests how many agents are at this node; If the number of agents at the node is at least $k - 1$, the algorithm terminates

---

In Algorithm 28, eventually, since all agents travel clockwise, all but one agent (which will vanish into the black hole) will be at the same node. In the worst case, this node will be adjacent to the black hole. Since using cautious walk, it takes 3 traversals to safely move one node clockwise, and since there are at most $n - 2$ such possible moves, we have:

Lemma 5.38   *Let k be the total number of dispersed agents in the ring and let k be known. Algorithm 28 lets $k - 1$ agents gather in an oriented ring with a black hole in at most $3n - 6$ moves.*

In view of Theorem 5.35, Algorithm 28 is size optimal.

n UNKNOWN, *k* KNOWN ODD NUMBER, UNORIENTED RING

Algorithm 29 solves rendezvous in an unoriented ring and when k is a known odd number. Following the algorithm, the agents are divided into two sets: 'clockwise' and 'counter-clockwise', where all agents in the same set have a common view of 'clockwise.' Notice that each agent, although anonymous, can easily detect whether a message on a whiteboard has been written by an agent in the same set or not (e.g., each message contains also an indication of which of the two local ports the writer considers to be 'clockwise').

Theorem 5.39   (40).   *Algorithm 29 terminates after at most $5(n - 2)$ moves gathering $k - 2$ agents.*

Algorithm 29 (Gr-Odd)

1: The agents of each set first of all execute Algorithm 28 for oriented rings, independently of and ignoring the agents of the other set, terminating as soon as $\frac{k-1}{2}$ agents of the same set gather in the same node. Call them *red* agents.

2: The node where the $\frac{k-1}{2}$ have gathered becomes the collection point and one of those agents is selected as left-collector.

3: Every other agent arriving at the collection point joins the group.

4: The left collector x travels (using cautious walk when necessary) counter-clockwise and tells every agent it encounters to go to the collection point; it does so until it reaches the black hole or the last safe node explored. In the latter case, the left collector leaves a message for agent y informing it of the meeting point and instructing it to become left collector, it then returns to the collection point. If and when agent y returns to that node, it finds the message, becomes left collector and acts accordingly.

5: A red agent returning to the collection point during its cautious walk becomes now a right collector.

6: The rules for the right collector are exactly those for the left collector, where 'left' is replaced by 'right' and vice-versa.

In view of Theorem 5.35, Algorithm 29 is size optimal.

We refer the interested reader to article (39) for other results concerning cases when k is an even number, or unknown in oriented and unoriented rings, etc.

5.8   COMMENTS AND BIBLIOGRAPHIC REMARKS

The study of rendezvous or gathering of anonymous identical robots has been studied extensively (1; 9; 17; 18; 19; 56; 82; 83; 91) and is closely related to Look-Compute-Move model considered above. For example, In (17; 18; 19; 56; 82; 83; 91) it was proved in (56) that gathering is possible in the asynchronous model if robots have the same orientation of the plane, even with limited visibility. Without orientation, the gathering problem was positively solved in (18), assuming that robots have the capability of multiplicity detection. A complementary negative result concerning the asynchronous model was proved in (83): without multiplicity detection, gathering robots that do not have orientation is impossible.

The same model has been assumed for studying the exploration problem under different topologies. In (49), the authors have studied ring exploration, showing that exploration of a ring of n nodes is unsolvable by k robots as long as k divides n. They also show that the minimum number $p(n)$ of robots that can explore a ring of size n is $O(\log n)$ and that $p(n) = \Omega(\log n)$ for arbitrarily large n.

In (50), the authors have used the same model studying tree exploration. They prove that there are n-node trees where $\Omega(n)$ robots are necessary, and this holds even if the maximum degree is 4. They also prove that if the maximum degree is 3 then $\Theta(\frac{\log n}{\log \log n})$ robots are needed and suffice for tree exploration.

In (16), the authors consider a very similar model. In fact, the only difference with the Look-Compute-Move model discussed above is that they assume the standard local orientation of the network. In other words, they model the network as an edge-labeled graph. They study the Gathering problem and the Exploration problem, and prove that $k = 2l + 1$ robots can gather in any connected graph with asymmetric placement in finite time. For the Exploration problem they show that while 3 robots cannot explore all graphs, $k = 2l + 1$ robots can explore any connected graph with asymmetric placement in finite time. In the ring topology, they prove that gathering and exploration problems are solvable regardless of the number $k > 2$ of robots if and only if their placement is asymmetric. the situation is the same on a tree with respect to the gathering problem while for the exploration problem $k \geq 4$ robots asymmetrically placed suffice.

An interesting extension is studied in (34) whereby they investigate the possibility of solving deterministically the gathering problem (GP) with weak (anonymous, autonomous, disoriented, deaf and dumb, and oblivious) robots. They introduce the concept of strong multiplicity detection as the ability for the robots to detect the exact number of robots located at a given position. They show that with strong multiplicity detection, there exists a deterministic self-stabilizing algorithm solving GP for n robots if, and only if, n is odd.

(30) solves rendezvous of k mobile agents carrying faulty tokens in n node asynchronous rings for arbitrary values of n and k, whenever it is solvable. Based on the ideas of the solution for ring networks, they also present a more complicated solution for the more general case, when the network topology is arbitrary and unknown. Their algorithm for solving rendezvous in this case requires $O(k\Delta^{2n})$ moves for graphs of maximum degree Δ. A related paper on rendezvous with faulty tokens in a ring is (28).

The Black Hole Search problem has been studied extensively in many types of asynchronous networks using the *whiteboard* model ((36; 37; 42; 41; 43; 44)). The problem has been also investigated in asynchronous networks using the token model in (38; 45; 47; 46; 48; 51; 90). The issue of efficient black hole search has been as well studied in synchronous networks without whiteboards or tokens in (20; 21; 26; 25; 65; 64; 87). The synchronous scenario makes a dramatic change to the problem of searching for a black hole. Now, it is possible to use the time-out mechanism to locate the black hole in any graph, with only two agents, as follows: agents proceed along edges of a spanning tree. If they are at a safe node v, one agent goes to the adjacent node and returns, while the other agent waits at v. If after 2 time units the first agent has not returned, the other one survives and knows the location of the black hole. Otherwise, the adjacent node is known to be safe and both agents can move to it. This time-out mechanism makes black hole search feasible in any graph without the need of whiteboards. In particular, the network does not have to be 2-connected anymore, as in asynchronous networks, and, furthermore, it is now possible to answer the question of whether a black hole actually exists or not in the network. Hence the issue in this case is not the feasibility but the time efficiency of black hole search. Finally, there are a few papers extending the work on rendezvous on dangerous networks described here ((40; 15; 52)).

CHAPTER 6

Other Topologies

6.1 INTRODUCTION

In a way, the less symmetric the graph is, the easier it is to solve the rendezvous problem. Intuitively, this is because the mobile agents can take advantage of asymmetries (e.g., existence of a distinguished node or edge or even a unique subgraph with a special structure) in order to rendezvous. In this chapter, we discuss in some detail rendezvous in a torus indicating an interesting interplay between symmetry, number of tokens being used and memory needed by the agents. In addition, we outline how rendezvous can be accomplished in arbitrary trees and general graphs.

6.2 SYNCHRONOUS TORUS

We keep here the same model as in Chapter 2 with the exception of the underlying graph topology. More specifically, our model consists of two anonymous and identical mobile agents that are placed in an anonymous, synchronous and oriented torus. The torus consists of n rings and each of these rings consists of m nodes. Since the torus is oriented, we can say that it consists of n vertical rings. A horizontal ring of the torus consists of n nodes while a vertical ring consists of m nodes. We call such a torus a $n \times m$ torus. The mobile agents share a common orientation of the torus, i.e., they agree on any direction (clockwise vertical or horizontal). Each mobile agent owns a number of identical tokens. The agents follow the same deterministic algorithm and begin execution at the same time and being at the same initial state.

We assume that the memory required by an agent is at least proportional to the number $\Theta(\log(\sigma))$ of bits required to encode its $\sigma \geq 2$ states. Memory permitting, an agent can count the number of nodes between tokens or the total number of nodes of the torus, etc. The agents have no knowledge about the number of nodes of the torus or any other parameter of the network, apart from its dimension.

Rendezvous occurs when the agents either meet on a network node or simultaneously cross the same network link while moving in opposite directions. We will discuss as in Chapter 2 *rendezvous without detection* ($\mathcal{RP}$) and *rendezvous with detection* ($\mathcal{RD}$).

The *distance* between two nodes (x_1, x_2) and (y_1, y_2) on a 2-dimensional torus $n \times m$, is a 2-dimensional vector (d_1, d_2) where $d_1 = \min\{|x_1 - y_1|, (n - |x_1 - y_1|)\}$ and $d_2 = \min\{|x_2 - y_2|, (m - |x_2 - y_2|)\}$. An example of two agents in a torus is shown in Figure 6.1.

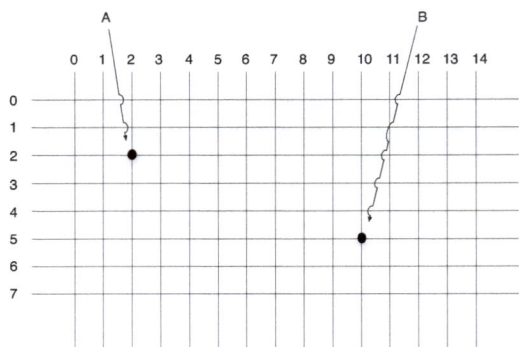

Figure 6.1: Two agents in a 15×8 (2–dimensional) torus. Agent A has coordinates $(2, 2)$. Agent B has coordinates $(10, 5)$. Their distance is $d(A, B) = (\min\{|A_1 - B_1|, (n - |A_1 - B_1|)\}, \min\{|A_2 - B_2|, (m - |A_2 - B_2|)\}) = (\min\{|2 - 10|, (15 - |2 - 10|)\}, \min\{|2 - 5|, (8 - |2 - 5|)\}) = (\min\{8, 7\}, \min\{3, 5\}) = (7, 3)$.

Theorem 6.1 (68). *Consider two identical agents placed in a 2-dimensional oriented torus ($n \times m$), so that their distance is either $(n/2, 0)$ (with n even) or $(0, m/2)$ (with m even) or $(n/2, m/2)$ (with n, m even). The agents start at the same initial state. Then, no matter how many tokens (movable or unmovable) or how much memory the agents have, it is impossible for the agents to rendezvous at a node or an edge.*

Proof. Let D be the initial distance of the agents, with $D = (n/2, 0)$ or $D = (0, m/2)$ or $D = (n/2, m/2)$. Since the agents start at the same state S_0, as long as they do not release tokens, they enter simultaneously the same state S_t at any time t, moving in the same direction, thus maintaining their initial distance. Hence, if they release a token, they do it at the same time t_k, being at the same state S_k and having the initial distance D. Thus the distance of the released tokens is also D, i.e. for any token t_A released by agent A, there is a token t_B released by agent B at distance D. At any time $t' > t_k$, as long as the agents do not meet tokens while they are moving in the same direction, they again, simultaneously, enter the same state $S_{t'}$ maintaining distance D. Now suppose that one of the agents, say A, meets a token while moving. Consider the following two cases:

i) Suppose that A meets token t_A, which had been released by A earlier (we remind here that all tokens are indistinguishable and hence, agent A is not aware that t_A has been released by him). In this case, since the agents were moving identically maintaining distance D, agent B must meet token t_B (which had been released by B earlier) at exactly the same time.

ii) Suppose that A meets token t_B (which had been released by B earlier) at time t_l. This means that at time t_i, agent A is at distance D from token t_A. Since up to that time t_l, the agents were moving identically (i.e., in the same direction, entering the same states and covering the same distance), agent B is at distance D from token t_B. But this is the position where token t_A lies. Hence, at time t_l, both agents meet tokens.

In other words, they are always simultaneously enter the same states; their configuration is the same (they both carry the same number of tokens) while the configuration of the node they occupy is always the same (no tokens or the same number of tokens). Therefore, since they act identically, they maintain their distance forever.   □

Theorem 6.1 is a generalization of Theorem 2.5 of Chapter 2, which states that it is impossible for two agents equipped with one unmovable token each, to rendezvous in a ring with n nodes if their initial distance is $n/2$, where n is even.

6.2.1   MEMORY LOWER BOUNDS FOR RENDEZVOUS

We present here lower bounds for the memory the agents need in order to rendezvous. Let us first discuss how many nodes of the torus an agent can visit.

Lemma 6.2   *Consider one mobile agent with $\sigma \geq 2$ states and no tokens. We can always (for any configuration of the automaton, i.e., states and transition function) select an $n \times n$ oriented torus, where $n > \sigma$ so that no matter what is the starting position of the agent, it cannot visit all nodes of the torus. In fact, the agent will visit at most $n(\sigma - 1) + 1$ nodes.*

Proof. If we select an oriented $n \times n$ torus, where $n > \sigma$ then the agent has to repeat a state at some point (before visiting all nodes). Let S be the first state repeated. Let $v = (v_x, v_y)$ be the node where the agent is located when S is encountered for the first time and v' be the node where the agent is located when S is repeated for the first time. We call p_x, p_y the horizontal and vertical distance, respectively, between v and v'. Since S is the first state repeated, the total number of nodes visited by the agent until it repeats S for the first time is at most $\sigma + 1$. In particular, the total number of nodes visited by the agent after the moment that first encountered S and until it enters S again (i.e., between visiting nodes v and v' without counting v) is at most $\sigma - 1$ (notice that the initial state S_0 occurs only in the beginning).

Once the agent is again at state S, it has to repeat the same trajectory (p_x, p_y) and visiting again at most $\sigma - 1$ new nodes until it encounters S again. Label the coordinates of the nodes of the torus $0, \ldots, n - 1$, horizontally and vertically. If v_x, v_y are the coordinates of node v, then after n repetitions of state S, the position of the agent is:

$$(v_x + np_x) \mod n = v_x$$

$$(v_y + np_y) \mod n = v_y$$

This means that the agent is again at node v and state S. The agent has to continue moving visiting exactly the same nodes. Up to that moment, the agent has visited at most $(\sigma + 1) + (n - 1)(\sigma - 1) - 1 = n(\sigma - 1) + 1 < n^2$ nodes.   □

Following similar arguments we can prove the lemma below.

Lemma 6.3   *Consider one mobile agent with $\sigma \geq 2$ states and one unmovable token. We can always (for any configuration of the automaton, i.e., states and transition function) select an oriented $n \times n$ torus, where $n > \sigma^2$ so that no matter what is the starting position of the agent, it cannot visit all nodes of the torus. In fact, the agent will visit at most $\sigma + (\sigma - 1)^2(n + 1) < n^2$ nodes.*

Now let us consider two agents on the torus. Based on the fact that an agent with one unmovable token can not visit all nodes of the ring (Lemma 6.3), the adversary can 'hide' token t_A in a node not visited by agent B and token t_B in a node not visited by agent A. Following this technique, we can show:

Lemma 6.4   *Consider two mobile agents with σ states and one unmovable token each. We can always (for any configuration of the automatons, i.e., states and transition function) place the agents in an $n \times n$ oriented torus, where $n > 2\sigma^2$ so that they cannot rendezvous.*

Contrary to the case of unmovable tokens, if the agents could move the tokens, then it is easy to think of an algorithm where all nodes of any torus can be visited by the same agent. For example consider the following algorithm for an agent with one movable token:

Algorithm 30

1: release the token at the starting node;
2: go right counting tokens until you meet the second token;
3: move the token down;
4: **repeat** from step 2;

Nevertheless, in the following scenario where the agents can move tokens, we again show that the adversary can place the agents in a way that they could meet and move only their own token.

Definition 6.5   If there are two starting nodes s, s' for the agents A and B so that agent A drops its token t_A in a node not visited by agent B and agent B drops its token t_B in a node not visited by agent A, then we say that s, s' satisfy property π.

Lemma 6.6   *Consider two mobile agents with σ states and one movable token each. We can always (for any configuration of the automatons, i.e., states and transition function) place the agents in an $n \times n$ oriented torus, where $n > 2\sigma^2$ so that they cannot rendezvous.*

Proof. In view of Lemma 6.4, as long as $n > 2\sigma^2$ the adversary can initially place the agents so that if they see a token, it is their own token (up to the moment that they decide to move it). Suppose that at some point, they decide to move their token. Since the agents are identical and start at the same state, they will visit their own token and take the decision to move it simultaneously. Since, up to that point, they have maintained their initial distance, they will again place their tokens maintaining the initial distance and their new starting positions also have the same distance as before and thus they continue to satisfy property π. Therefore, they will never meet each other. ☐

This implies the following theorem:

Theorem 6.7 (68). *Two agents with one movable token each, need at least $\Omega(\log n)$ memory to solve the RV problem in a $n \times n$ oriented torus.*

Proof. Suppose that the agents have a memory of r bits. Hence they can have at most $\sigma = 2^r$ states. By Lemma 6.6 as long as $n > 2\sigma^2$ the agents cannot rendezvous. Hence, the agents need at least $r = \Omega(\log n)$ memory to rendezvous. ☐

6.2.2   RENDEZVOUS ALGORITHMS

In this section, we prove that $O(\log n + \log m)$ memory is enough for the agents equipped with one unmovable token each, in order to achieve rendezvous with detection in an arbitrary $n \times m$ oriented torus. Therefore, both $\mathcal{RP}$ and $\mathcal{RD}$ problems require $\Theta(\log n + \log m)$ memory in an arbitrary $n \times m$ oriented torus when the agents have one (movable or unmovable) token each.

We further investigate the situation when the agents have two movable tokens and constant memory each and we show that in this case $\mathcal{RD}$ can be solved in a $n \times n$ oriented torus.

RENDEZVOUS WITH DETECTION ($\mathcal{RD}$) IN A $n \times m$ TORUS WITH $O(\log n + \log m)$ MEMORY

We first describe an algorithm which solves the $\mathcal{RD}$ problem of two agents equipped with one unmovable token and $O(\log n + \log m)$ memory each in any $n \times m$ oriented torus. We remind the reader that the agents do not know n or m, but as we will see, they can use their memory to calculate them. Below is a high-level description of the algorithm (Algorithm 31).

First, the agent (both agents run the same algorithm) moves in the initial horizontal ring; it releases its token and counts steps until it meets a token twice. If its counters (measuring inter-token distances) differ, then rendezvous can be arranged. Otherwise, it does the same in the initial vertical ring. If it does not meet the other agent, then it searches one by one the horizontal rings of the torus counting its steps. If it meets a token while going down passing from one horizontal ring to the other, then it declares that rendezvous is impossible. Otherwise, if it meets a token while going right in an horizontal ring (which means that the agents must have started in different rings), then: If at least one of its counters counting horizontal or vertical distances from its token is different than $n/2$ or $m/2$, respectively, then rendezvous can be arranged. Otherwise, it stops and declares that rendezvous is impossible.

Algorithm 31 Algorithm for $\mathcal{RD}$ in a $n \times m$ oriented torus with 1 unmovable token and $O(\log n + \log m)$ memory

---

1: SameRing
2: DifRing

As Algorithm 31 suggests, the agents first execute Procedure SameRing. If they do not meet each other, then either they must have started in symmetrical positions in the same ring or they must have started in different rings. In any of those cases, they execute Procedure DifRing. Their exploration finishes after at most $O(nm)$ steps, while they need $O(\log n + \log m)$ memory for counting.

Procedure SameRing

1: leave your token down
2: go right and count steps until you see a token
3: $c_1 \leftarrow$ this number of steps
4: go right and count steps until you see a token
5: $c_2 \leftarrow$ this number of steps
6: **if** $c_2 \neq c_1$ **then**
7:    Rendezvous(horizontal, c_1, c_2)
8: **else**
9:    go down and count steps until you see a token
10:    $c_3 \leftarrow$ this number of steps
11:    go down and count steps until you see a token
12:    $c_4 \leftarrow$ this number of steps.
13:    **if** $c_4 \neq c_3$ **then**
14:       Rendezvous(vertical, c_3, c_4)
15:    **end if**
16: **end if**

Lemma 6.8 *If the agents are located on the same ring of a $n \times m$ oriented torus in non-symmetrical positions, then Procedure SameRing will lead them to rendezvous.*

Proof. After $c_1 + c_2$ steps the agents see their token. So they are again located at their starting positions. If $c_1 \neq c_2$, this means that the agents started in the same horizontal ring. They execute Procedure Rendezvous on the horizontal ring and rendezvous. If $c_2 = c_1$, then the agents must

Procedure Rendezvous(ring, c_1, c_2)

1: **if** ring $=$ horizontal **then**
2:     **if** $c_2 > c_1$ **then**
3:         go right
4:     **else**
5:         go left
6:     **end if**
7: **end if**
8: **if** ring $=$ vertical **then**
9:     **if** $c_2 > c_1$ **then**
10:        go down
11:    **else**
12:        go up
13:    **end if**
14: **end if**

---

have started in the same vertical ring. After $c_3 + c_4$ steps down, they meet their token on the vertical ring with $c_3 \neq c_4$. They execute Procedure Rendezvous on the vertical ring and rendezvous.   □

In view of Lemma 6.8, if after executing Procedure SameRing, the agents do not meet each other, then either they have started in the same ring in symmetrical positions or they have started in different rings. In any such case, it must hold $c_1 = c_2$ and $c_3 = c_4$.

Lemma 6.9   *If the agents are located on the same ring on symmetrical positions or in different rings of an oriented $n \times m$ torus, then Procedure DifRing is a $\mathcal{RD}$ algorithm.*

Proof. The agents explore one by one the other horizontal rings, first going down and then at most $2c_1$ steps to the right. If they first find a token while going down (passing from one horizontal ring to the next), then this token it is either their token (which means that they have started in the same horizontal ring) or the other's token (which means that they have started in the same vertical ring). In either of these cases, they declare that rendezvous is impossible. If they first find a token while going right in an horizontal ring then, having counted the distance to the right (c_5) and down (c_6) between their starting position and that token, if $c_5 \neq c_1/2$ or $c_6 \neq c_3/2$, they can easily break symmetries following Procedure Rendezvous2 and rendezvous. Otherwise, (when $c_5 = c_1/2$ and $c_6 = c_3/2$) they declare that rendezvous is impossible.   □

An example has been illustrated in Figure 6.2. Algorithm 31 together with Lemmas 6.8, 6.9 imply the following theorem.

Theorem 6.10   (68).   *The Rendezvous with Detection problem on an oriented $n \times m$ torus can be solved by two agents using one unmovable token and $O(\log n + \log m)$ memory each, in time $O(nm)$.*

Procedure DifRing

1: **repeat**
2:    go down to the next horizontal ring
3:    **repeat**
4:       go right
5:       $c_5 \leftarrow$ the number of steps right
6:    **until** $(c_5 = 2c_1)$ OR (you meet a token)
7: **until** you meet a token
8: $c_6 \leftarrow$ the number of rings down
9: **if** (you have met a token while going down) **then**
10:    stop and declare rendezvous impossible
11: **else**
12:    **if** $c_6 \neq c_3/2$ **then**
13:       Rendezvous2$(c_6, c_3/2)$
14:    **else**
15:       **if** $c_5 \neq c_1/2$ **then**
16:          Rendezvous2$(c_5, c_1/2)$
17:       **else**
18:          stop and declare rendezvous impossible
19:       **end if**
20:    **end if**
21: **end if**

Procedure Rendezvous2(ct, ck)

1: **if** $ct < ck$ **then**
2:    reverse horizontal direction and go c_5 horizontally and then vertically until you meet your token and wait
3: **end if**
4: **if** $ct > ck$ **then**
5:    wait
6: **end if**

RENDEZVOUS WITH DETECTION ($\mathcal{RD}$) IN A $n \times n$ TORUS WITH CONSTANT MEMORY

We now give an algorithm which solves the $\mathcal{RD}$ problem for two agents equipped with two movable tokens each and constant memory in any square anonymous, synchronous and oriented torus.

We first define Procedures HorScan and VerScan which will be used in our algorithms.

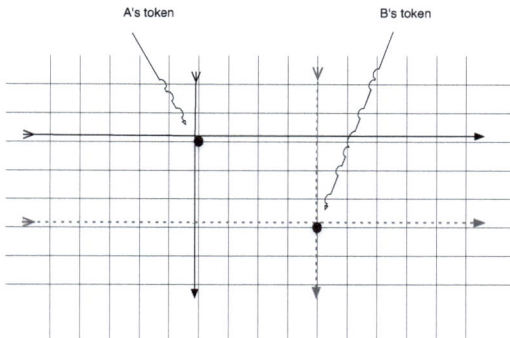

Figure 6.2: Two agents with $O(\log n + \log m)$ memory and one unmovable token each.

Procedure HorScan

1: **repeat**
2:    go down, right, up
3: **until** you meet a token

Procedure VerScan

1: **repeat**
2:    go right, down, left
3: **until** you meet a token

In these procedures, the agent stops immediately after it meets a token. So for example, if it executes Procedure HorScan and then, after it goes right, it meets a token then it stops immediately; it does not go up. We also use Procedure FindTokenHor:

An agent following Procedure FindTokenHor, scans one by one the horizontal rings of the torus until it meets a token while moving down or right. Below, we explain Procedure FindTokenHor and prove some of its properties.

Let the agents release their first token at their starting positions and execute Procedure FindTokenHor. During execution of HorScan (step 2 of Procedure FindTokenHor), the agent has to meet a token for the first time either after it moved down in the first step, or up or right (it can not meet a token while going down at a later step of HorScan since it would have met the token while going right earlier).

If it meets a token after it moved up, then this can be any token: its own first token or the other's first token (or its own second token or the other's second token when it scans a later horizontal ring). However, if it executes Procedure HorScan again (step 4 of Procedure FindTokenHor), then

---

Procedure FindTokenHor

1: **repeat**
2:     HorScan
3:     **if** you meet token up **then**
4:         HorScan
5:         go one step down and drop (or move) the second token
6:     **end if**
7: **until** you meet a token down or right
8: **if** you meet a token down **then**
9:     SameRing:=1
10: **else**
11:     SameRing:=0
12: **end if**

---

no matter what was the case, it is easy to see that the first token it meets now is its token (first or second) and it meets it after it moved up (supposing that there are at most two tokens in the same horizontal ring). Furthermore, in this case, it is sure that the down horizontal ring had no tokens.

If it meets a token while going right, then it is clear that it is the other's first token, and that the two agents have started in different rings.

If it meets a token while it goes down then either it is its first token or the other's first token. In both cases this means that they have started in the same ring: if it is its first token it means that it has searched the whole torus and did not meet any other token while it was moving right.

Therefore, the agent exits Procedure FindTokenHor knowing that it has started either in the same ring with the other agent (if it met a token after it moved down) or in different rings (if it met a token after it moved right).

We also use Procedure FindTokenVer which scans one by one the vertical rings of the torus using Procedure VerScan. Procedure FindTokenVer has exactly the same properties with Procedure FindTokenHor if we replace direction down with right, right with down and up with left. If we had a guarantee that the agents started in different rings then an agent executing Procedure FindTokenVer, it will exit the procedure, meeting a token while it moves down. The movements of the agents following these two procedures are shown in Figure 6.3. Both procedures FindTokenHor and FindTokenVer need $O(n^2)$ time units.

We also use Algorithm 7 from Chapter 2 which solves rendezvous with detection in a ring using two agents with two tokens and constant memory each.

Combining those procedures we now give the main Procedure SearchTorus that will be used in Algorithm 32 which is a $\mathcal{RD}$ algorithm for two agents with constant memory in a $n \times n$ oriented torus. A high-level description of the Procedure SearchTorus is the following:

The two agents search one by one the horizontal rings of the torus (using Procedure FindTokenHor) to discover whether they have started in the same ring. If so, then they get syn-

Procedure FindTokenVer

1: **repeat**
2:    VerScan
3:    **if** you meet token left **then**
4:       VerScan
5:       go one step right and drop (or move) the second token
6:    **end if**
7: **until** you meet a token down

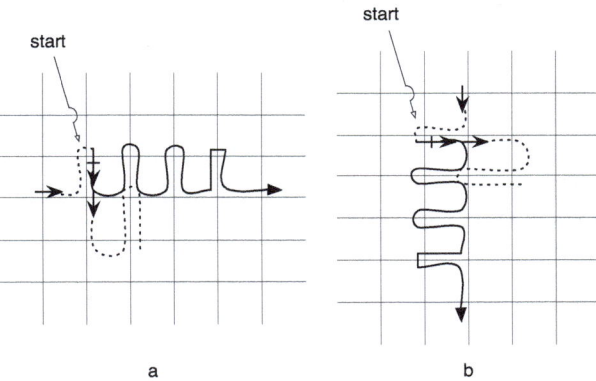

a   b

Figure 6.3: a) An agent executing Procedure `FindTokenHor` and b) an agent executing Procedure `FindTokenVer`.

chronized (i.e., they go at the same time, back at their starting nodes) and they execute Algorithm 7 from Chapter 2. Otherwise they try to 'catch' each other on the torus using a path, marked by their tokens. If they do not rendezvous, then they get synchronized and search one by one the vertical rings of the torus (using Procedure `FindTokenVer`). They again try to 'catch' each other on the torus. If they do not meet this time, they declare rendezvous impossible. Algorithm 32 takes $O(n^2)$ time.

This leads to the following theorem.

Theorem 6.11 (68). *The Rendezvous with Detection problem on a $n \times n$ oriented torus can be solved by two agents using two movable tokens and constant memory each, in time $O(n^2)$.*

The interested reader may find the details of the proof of Theorem 6.11 in (68).

We conclude this section with the following observations.

In a torus, it appears that there is a strict hierarchy on the power of tokens and memory with respect to rendezvous: a constant number of unmovable tokens are less powerful than two

---

Procedure SearchTorus

1: release the first token
2: FindTokenHor
3: **if** SameRing **then**
4:    Synchronize
5:    Algorithm 7 from Chapter 2 on the horizontal ring
6:    Algorithm 7 on the vertical ring
7:    **if** not rendezvous **then**
8:       stop and declare rendezvous impossible
9:    **end if**
10: **else**
11:    go up until you meet a token
12:    go one step down
13:    **repeat**
14:       go left, wait 1 time step
15:    **until** (rendezvous) OR (you meet a token for the second time)
16:    **if** not rendezvous **then**
17:       Synchronize
18:       FindTokenVer
19:       go left until you meet a token
20:       go one step right
21:       **repeat**
22:          go up, wait 1 time step
23:       **until** (rendezvous) OR (you meet a token for the second time)
24:    **end if**
25: **end if**

Algorithm 32 RVD2n

1: SearchTorus
2: **if** not rendezvous **then**
3:    stop and declare rendezvous impossible
4: **end if**

---

movable tokens. While the hierarchy collapses on three tokens (an algorithm for rendezvous with detection in a $n \times m$ torus when the agents have constant memory each has been presented in (68)), it remains an open question if three tokens are strictly more powerful than two with respect to rendezvous with detection. Another interesting open problem on the number of tokens needed for solving rendezvous with or without detection having constant memory, arises when the torus is not oriented. We conjecture that by using additional tokens one may be able to extend the algorithms of this section to the case of the unoriented torus.

6.3   TREES

The discussion in this section concerns rendezvous of two mobile agents (without tokens) in a synchronous tree. In this case, a solution exists if and only if the initial positions of the agents are not symmetric and is based on the work of (57). There it is shown that the minimum memory size guaranteeing rendezvous in all trees of size at most n is $\Theta(\log n)$ bits. The upper bound accomplishes rendezvous in all trees of size at most n using $O(\log n)$ bits of memory while the lower bound follows from the fact that one needs to distinguish between up to $n - 1$ links incident to a node. This paper also addresses the potential existence of pairs of mobile agents that can accomplish rendezvous in all bounded degree trees by showing that there are no finite agents capable of accomplishing rendezvous in all bounded degree trees.

The nodes of the trees are unlabeled, while edges incident to a node have distinct ports (or labels), where the number of ports is equal to the degree of the node. Every undirected edge has two labels one for each node of the edge. The port numbering is local in the sense that there is no relation between port numbers at different nodes. A pair of nodes of the tree is called symmetric if there exists an automorphism (formally, an automorphism $f : V \to V$ is a bijection of the vertex set V of the tree) carrying one node to the other and which preserves the port numbering.

Mobile agents are traversing the trees performing actions in rounds measured by an internal clock and are modeled as usual using automata. It is easy to see that if the initial positions are not symmetric then there exists a pair of agents that can meet in a given tree. The argument is simple and runs as follows. Consider an arbitrary tree. Trees are known to have either a central node or a central edge.

- If the tree has a central node then two agents equipped with sufficient memory can meet at this central node, regardless of the initial position.

- If the tree has a central edge, then for non-symmetric initial positions one of the endpoints of the central edge can be distinguished from the other, and agents will meet there.

- Finally, for a symmetric initial position in a tree with a central edge, if the agents start simultaneously they will never meet, as all their actions will be symmetric with respect to this central edge.

Two types of rendezvous are being defined: 1) *rendezvous without termination* whereby it is not specified what happens if the agents never meet, in which case they may wander in the tree indefinitely, and 2) *rendezvous with termination* whereby agents either eventually meet (one of the agents may join later the other that first stopped), or each of them stops in the final state at different nodes detecting that rendezvous is impossible. The main result is summarized in the following theorem.

Theorem 6.12 (57).

1. *There exist two identical mobile agents accomplishing rendezvous with termination in all trees, and using, for any integer n, $O(\log n)$ bits of memory in trees of size at most n.*

2. *For any pair of identical mobile agents, there is a line on which these agents cannot accomplish rendezvous, even without termination.*

For additional details on the proof, the reader is advised to consult the original paper (57) mentioned above.

6.4 ARBITRARY GRAPHS

The rendezvous problem for a more general class of graphs (simple undirected connected network with local port labelings but without node labels) is studied in (33). In this version of the problem, the two mobile agents have arbitrary startup times, or even starting times arbitrarily decided by an adversary and are assumed to have unique positive integer labels.

Before we state the main results of this paper we introduce some basic notation. The difference between startup times of the agents is denoted by τ. The agents have labels denoted by L_1, L_2 and let ℓ be the smallest of the two labels. For a given graph, n denotes the number of nodes, and Δ is the maximum degree of a node. Moreover D denotes the distance between initial positions of agents. The agent with the earlier startup is called the *earlier* agent and the other agent is called the *later* agent. In the case of simultaneous startup, the earlier agent is defined as agent 1. (An agent does not know if it is earlier or later.)

The paper analyzes the rendezvous problem in this setting for trees, rings and arbitrary graphs. The main theorem is as follows.

Theorem 6.13 (33). *The following results hold for two mobile agents.*

1. *There is an algorithm that performs rendezvous on any n-node tree in $O(n + \log \ell)$ steps. Moreover, there exist n-node trees on which any rendezvous algorithm requires cost $\Omega(n + \log \ell)$, even with simultaneous startup.*

2. *In the simultaneous startup model the minimum cost of rendezvous in the ring is $\Theta(D \log \ell)$. Moreover, in the arbitrary startup model the minimum cost of rendezvous in the n-node ring is $\Omega(n + D \log \ell)$.*

3. *In arbitrary graphs with simultaneous startup, rendezvous can be accomplished in $O(D \Delta^D \log \ell)$ steps.*

For additional details on the proof the reader is advised to consult the original paper (33) mentioned above.

6.5 COMMENTS AND BIBLIOGRAPHIC REMARKS

A related paper on asynchronous rendezvous in arbitrary graphs is (27). In this paper, the authors prove that two mobile agents with distinct labels can rendezvous in any arbitrary, possibly infinite, unknown and asynchronous graph by using deterministic algorithms. They also study the rendezvous problem in geometric scenarios. Another line of research for multiple agent rendezvous comes from control theory. One wants to devise "local" control strategies, which without any active communication between robots, cause all members of the group to eventually rendezvous at a single unspecified location (72; 74; 73).

Bibliography

[1] N. Agmon and D. Peleg. Fault-tolerant gathering algorithms for autonomous mobile robots. *SIAM Journal on Computing*, 36(1):56–82, 2006. DOI: 10.1137/050645221 73

[2] G. L. Alexanderson. *The random walks of George Pólya*. The Mathematical Association of America, 2000. 40

[3] S. Alpern. The rendezvous search problem. *SIAM Journal of Control and Optimization*, 33:673–683, 1995. DOI: 10.1137/S0363012993249195 26, 38

[4] S. Alpern. Rendezvous in one and more dimensions. Technical report, The London School of Economics, 2001. 26

[5] S. Alpern. Rendezvous search: A personal perspective. *Operations Research*, 50(5):772–795, 2002. DOI: 10.1287/opre.50.5.772.363 26

[6] S. Alpern and S. Gal. Rendezvous search on the line with distinguishable players. *SIAM Journal Control and Optimization*, 33:1270–1276, 1995. DOI: 10.1137/S0363012993260288 26

[7] S. Alpern and S. Gal. Searching for an agent who may or may not want to be found. *Operations Research*, 50(2):311–323, 2002. DOI: 10.1287/opre.50.2.311.433 26

[8] S. Alpern and S. Gal. *The Theory of Search Games and Rendezvous*. Kluwer Academic Publishers, 2003. 8, 26

[9] H. Ando, Y. Oasa, I. Suzuki, and M. Yamashita. A distributed memoryless point convergence algorithm for mobile robots with limited visibility. *I.E.E.E. Transactions on Robotics and Animation*, 15(5):818–828, 1999. DOI: 10.1109/70.795787 8, 73

[10] T. M. Apostol. *Introduction to Analytical Number Theory*. Springer Verlag, 1997. 19

[11] H. Attiya, M. Snir, and M. K. Warmuth. Computing on an anonymous ring. *Journal of the ACM*, 35(4):845–875, 1988. DOI: 10.1145/48014.48247 6

[12] L. Barriere, P. Flocchini, P. Fraigniaud, and N. Santoro. Rendezvous and election of mobile agents: impact of sense of direction. *Theory of Computing Systems*, 40(2):143–162, 2007. DOI: 10.1007/s00224-005-1223-5 28

[13] V. Baston and S. Gal. Rendezvous on the line when the players' initial distance is given by an unknown probability distribution. *SIAM Journal of Control and Optimization*, 36(6):1880–1889, 1998. DOI: 10.1137/S0363012996314130 26

[14] V. Baston and S. Gal. Rendezvous search when marks are left at the starting points. *Naval Research Logistics*, 47(6):722–731, 2001. DOI: 10.1002/nav.1044 7, 26

[15] J. Chalopin, S. Das, and N. Santoro. Rendezvous of mobile agents in unknown graphs with faulty links. In *Proceedings of 21st International Conference on Distributed Computing*, pages 108–122, 2007. DOI: 10.1007/978-3-540-75142-7_11 75

[16] J. Chalopin, P. Flocchini, B. Mans, and N. Santoro. Gathering and rendezvous by oblivious robots in arbitrary graphs, rings, and trees. Technical report, University of Ottawa, 2009. 74

[17] M. Cieliebak. Gathering non-oblivious mobile robots. In *Proceedings of 6th Latin American Theoretical Informatics Symposium*, LNCS 2976, pages 577–588, 2004. 73

[18] M. Cieliebak, P. Flocchini, G. Prencipe, and N. Santoro. Solving the robots gathering problem. In *Proceedings of 30th International Colloquium on Automata, Languages and Programming*, LNCS 2719, pages 1181–1196, 2003. DOI: 10.1007/3-540-45061-0_90 73

[19] R. Cohen and D. Peleg. Robot convergence via center-of-gravity algorithms. In *Proceedings of 11th International Colloquium on Structural Information and Communication Complexity*, LNCS 3104, pages 79–88, 2004. 73

[20] C. Cooper, R. Klasing, and T. Radzik. Searching for black-hole faults in a network using multiple agents. In *Proceedings of 10th International Conference on Principles of Distributed Systems*, LNCS 4305, pages 320–332, 2006. DOI: 10.1007/11945529_23 74

[21] C. Cooper, R. Klasing, and T. Radzik. Locating and repairing faults in a network with mobile agents. In *Proceedings of International Colloquium on Structural Information and Communication Complexity*, LNCS 5058, pages 20–32, 2008. DOI: 10.1007/978-3-540-69355-0_4 74

[22] D. Coppersmith, P. Tetali, and P. Winkler. Collisions among random walks on a graph. *SIAM Journal of Discrete Mathematics*, 6:363–374, 1993. DOI: 10.1137/0406029 40

[23] T. H. Cormen, C. E. Leiserson, R. L. Rivest, and C. Stein. *Introduction to Algorithms*. The MIT press, 2001. 19

[24] J. Czyzowicz, S. Dobrev, E. Kranakis, and D. Krizanc. The power of tokens: Rendezvous and symmetry detection for two mobile agents in a ring. In *Proceedings of 34th International Conference on Current Trends in Theory and Practice of Computer Science*, LNCS 4910, pages 234–246, 2008. DOI: 10.1007/978-3-540-77566-9_20 21, 23, 24, 26

[25] J. Czyzowicz, D. Kowalski, E. Markou, and A. Pelc. Complexity of searching for a black hole. *Fundamenta Informaticae*, 71(2-3):229–242, 2006. 74

[26] J. Czyzowicz, D. Kowalski, E. Markou, and A. Pelc. Searching for a black hole in synchronous tree networks. *Combinatorics, Probability & Computing*, 16(4):595–619, 2007. DOI: 10.1017/S0963548306008133 74

[27] J. Czyzowicz, A. Labourel, and A. Pelc. How to meet asynchronously (almost) everywhere. In *Proceedings of 21st Annual ACM-SIAM Symposium on Discrete Algorithms*, pages 22–30, 2010. 91

[28] S. Das. Mobile agent rendezvous in a ring using faulty tokens. In *Proceedings of 9th International Conference in Distributed Computing and Networking*, LNCS 4904, pages 292–297, 2008. DOI: 10.1007/978-3-540-77444-0_29 74

[29] S. Das, P. Flocchini, S. Kutten, A. Nayak, and N. Santoro. Map construction of unknown graphs by multiple agents. *Theoretical Computer Science*, 385(1-3):34–48, 2007. DOI: 10.1016/j.tcs.2007.05.011 33

[30] S. Das, M. Mihalak, R. Sramek, E. Vicari, and P. Widmayer. Rendezvous of mobile agents when tokens fail anytime. In *Proceedings of 12th International Conference on Principles of Distributed Systems*, LNCS 5401, pages 463–480, 2008. DOI: 10.1007/978-3-540-92221-6_29 74

[31] G. De Marco, L. Gargano, E. Kranakis, D. Krizanc, A. Pelc, and U. Vacaro. Asynchronous deterministic rendezvous in graphs. *Theoretical Computer Science*, 355:315–326, 2006. DOI: 10.1016/j.tcs.2005.12.016 53, 54, 55

[32] X. Deng and C. H. Papadimitriou. Exploring an unknown graph. *Journal of Graph Theory*, 32(3):265–297, 1999. DOI: 10.1002/(SICI)1097-0118(199911)32:3%3C265::AID-JGT6%3E3.0.CO;2-8 8

[33] A. Dessmark, P. Fraigniaud, D. R. Kowalski, and A. Pelc. Deterministic rendezvous in graphs. *Algorithmica*, 46(1):69–96, 2006. DOI: 10.1007/s00453-006-0074-2 90

[34] Y. Dieudonne and F. Petit. Self-stabilizing deterministic gathering. In *Proceedings of 5th International Workshop on Algorithmic Aspects of Wireless Sensor Networks*, LNCS 5804, pages 230–241, 2009. DOI: 10.1007/978-3-642-05434-1_23 74

[35] K. Diks, P. Fraigniaud, E. Kranakis, and A. Pelc. Tree exploration with little memory. *Journal of Algorithms*, 51:38–63, 2004. DOI: 10.1016/j.jalgor.2003.10.002 8

[36] S. Dobrev, P. Flocchini, R. Kralovic, G. Prencipe, P. Ruzicka, and N. Santoro. Black hole search by mobile agents in hypercubes and related networks. In *Proceedings of 6th International Conference on Principles of Distributed Systems*, pages 171–182, 2002. 74

[37] S. Dobrev, P. Flocchini, R. Kralovic, G. Prencipe, P. Ruzicka, and N. Santoro. Optimal search for a black hole in common interconnection networks. *Networks*, 47(2):61–71, 2006. DOI: 10.1002/net.20095 74

[38] S. Dobrev, P. Flocchini, R. Kralovic, and N. Santoro. Exploring a dangerous unknown graph using tokens. In *Proceedings of 5th IFIP International Conference on Theoretical Computer Science*, pages 131–150, 2006. DOI: 10.1007/978-0-387-34735-6_14 74

[39] S. Dobrev, P. Flocchini, G. Prencipe, and N. Santoro. Mobile agents search for a black-hole in an anonymous ring. In *Proceedings of 15th International Symposium on Distributed Computing*, pages 166–179, 2001. DOI: 10.1007/s00453-006-1232-z 68, 69, 71, 73

[40] S. Dobrev, P. Flocchini, G. Prencipe, and N. Santoro. Multiple agents rendezvous in a ring in spite of a black hole. In *Proceedings of 6th International Conference on Principles of Distributed Systems*, pages 34–46, 2003. 71, 72, 75

[41] S. Dobrev, P. Flocchini, G. Prencipe, and N. Santoro. Searching for a black hole in arbitrary networks: Optimal mobile agents protocols. *Distributed Computing*, 19(1):1–19, 2006. DOI: 10.1007/s00446-006-0154-y 74

[42] S. Dobrev, P. Flocchini, G. Prencipe, and N. Santoro. Mobile search for a black hole in an anonymous ring. *Algorithmica*, 48:67–90, 2007. 74

[43] S. Dobrev, P. Flocchini, and N. Santoro. Improved bounds for optimal black hole search in a network with a map. In *Proceedings of 10th International Colloquium on Structural Information and Communication Complexity*, pages 111–122, 2004. 74

[44] S. Dobrev, P. Flocchini, and N. Santoro. Cycling through a dangerous network: A simple efficient strategy for black hole search. In *Proceedings of International Conference on Distributed Computing Systems*, pages 57–65, 2006. DOI: 10.1109/ICDCS.2006.25 74

[45] S. Dobrev, R. Kralovic, N. Santoro, and W. Shi. Black hole search in asynchronous rings using tokens. In *Proceedings of 6th Conference on Algorithms and Complexity*, pages 139–150, 2006. DOI: 10.1007/11758471_16 74

[46] S. Dobrev, N. Santoro, and W. Shi. Locating a black hole in an un-oriented ring using tokens: The case of scattered agents. In *Proceedings of International European Conference on Parallel and Distributed Computing*, LNCS 4641, pages 608–617, 2007. DOI: 10.1007/978-3-540-74466-5_64 74

[47] S. Dobrev, N. Santoro, and W. Shi. Scattered black hole search in an oriented ring using tokens. In *Proceedings of IEEE International Parallel and Distributed Processing Symposium*, pages 1–8, 2007. DOI: 10.1109/IPDPS.2007.370460 74

[48] S. Dobrev, N. Santoro, and W. Shi. Using scattered mobile agents to locate a black hole in an un-oriened ring with tokens. *International Journal of Foundations of Computer Science*, 19(6):1355–1372, 2008. DOI: 10.1142/S0129054108006327 74

[49] P. Flocchini, D. Ilcinkas, A. Pelc, and N. Santoro. Computing without communicating: Ring exploration by asynchronous oblivious robots. In *Proceedings of 11th International Conference on Principles of Distributed Systems*, LNCS 4878, pages 105–118, 2007. DOI: 10.1007/978-3-540-77096-1_8 73

[50] P. Flocchini, D. Ilcinkas, A. Pelc, and N. Santoro. Remembering without memory: Tree exploration by asynchronous oblivious robots. In *Proceedings of 15th International Colloquium on Structural Information and Communication Complexity*, LNCS 5058, pages 33–47, 2008. DOI: 10.1007/978-3-540-69355-0_5 73

[51] P. Flocchini, D. Ilcinkas, and N. Santoro. Ping pong in dangerous graphs: Optimal black hole search with pure tokens. In *Proceedings of 22nd International Symposium on Distributed Computing*, LNCS 5218, pages 227–241, 2008. DOI: 10.1007/978-3-540-87779-0_16 74

[52] P. Flocchini, M. Kellett, P. Mason, and N. Santoro. Map construction and exploration by mobile agents scattered in a dangerous network. In *Proceedings of IEEE International Symposium on Parallel & Distributed Processing*, pages 1–10, 2009. DOI: 10.1109/IPDPS.2009.5161080 75

[53] P. Flocchini, E. Kranakis, D. Krizanc, F. Luccio, N. Santoro, and C. Sawchuk. Mobile agent rendezvous when tokens fail. In *Proceedings of 11th International Colloquium on Structural Information and Communication Complexity*, LNCS 3104, pages 161–172, 2004. DOI: 10.1007/b98251 44, 45, 47, 49

[54] P. Flocchini, E. Kranakis, D. Krizanc, N. Santoro, and C. Sawchuk. Multiple mobile agent rendezvous in the ring. In *Proceedings of 6th Latin American Theoretical Informatics Symposium*, pages 599–608, 2004. DOI: 10.1007/b95852 28, 29, 30, 32, 33, 41, 43

[55] P. Flocchini, B. Mans, and N. Santoro. Sense of direction: Definitions, properties, and classes. *Networks*, 32(3):165–180, 1998. DOI: 10.1002/(SICI)1097-0037(199810)32:3%3C165::AID-NET1%3E3.0.CO;2-I 5

[56] P. Flocchini, G. Prencipe, N. Santoro, and P. Widmayer. Gathering of asynchronous robots with limited visibility. *Theoretical Computer Science*, 337(1-3):147–168, 2005. DOI: 10.1016/j.tcs.2005.01.001 55, 73

[57] P. Fraigniaud and A. Pelc. Deterministic rendezvous in trees with little memory. In *Proceedings of 22nd International Symposium on Distributed Computing*, LNCS 5318, pages 242–256, 2008. DOI: 10.1007/978-3-540-87779-0_17 89, 90

[58] L. Gasieniec, E. Kranakis, D. Krizanc, and X. Zhang. Optimal memory rendezvous of anonymous mobile agents in a uni-directional ring. In *Proceedings of 32nd International Conference on Current Trends in Theory and Practice of Computer Science*, LNCS 3831, pages 282–292, 2006. DOI: 10.1007/11611257_26 33

[59] B. Hayes. The teetotaler's walk. *Bit-Player (web resource)*, February 2010. 40

[60] D. Hilbert. Mathematical problems. *Bulletin of American Mathematical Society*, 8(10):437–479, 1903. DOI: 10.1090/S0002-9904-1902-00923-3 ix

[61] L. M. Kirousis, E. Kranakis, and D. Krizanc. Rendezvous with flickering tokens, 2005. Unpublished manuscript. 51

[62] R. Klasing, A. Kosowski, and A. Navarra.   Taking advantage of symmetries: Gathering of asynchronous oblivious robots on a ring.   In *Proceedings of 12th International Conference on Principles of Distributed Systems*, LNCS 5401, pages 446–462, 2008. DOI: 10.1007/978-3-540-92221-6_28 67

[63] R. Klasing, E. Markou, and A. Pelc. Gathering asynchronous oblivious mobile robots in a ring. *Theoretical Computer Science*, 390:27–39, 2008. DOI: 10.1016/j.tcs.2007.09.032 60, 64

[64] R. Klasing, E. Markou, T. Radzik, and F. Sarracco. Hardness and approximation results for black hole search in arbitrary graphs. *Theoretical Computer Science*, 384(2-3):201–221, 2007. DOI: 10.1016/j.tcs.2007.04.024 74

[65] R. Klasing, E. Markou, T. Radzik, and F. Sarracco. Approximation bounds for black hole search problems. *Networks*, 52(4):216–226, 2008. DOI: 10.1002/net.20233 74

[66] D. Knuth. *The Art of Computer Programming, Volume 1: Fundamental Algorithms*. Addison-Wesley, 1997. 26

[67] E. Kranakis and D. Krizanc.   An algorithmic theory of mobile agents.   In *Proceedings of 2nd Symposium on Trustworthy Global Computing*, LNCS 4661, pages 86–97, 2007. DOI: 10.1007/978-3-540-75336-0_6 36

[68] E. Kranakis, D. Krizanc, and E. Markou. Mobile agent rendezvous in a synchronous torus. In *Proceedings of 7th Latin American Theoretical Informatics Symposium*, LNCS 3887, pages 653–664, 2006. DOI: 10.1007/11682462_60 78, 81, 83, 87, 88

[69] E. Kranakis, D. Krizanc, and P. Morin. Randomized Rendez-Vous with Limited Memory. In *Proceedings of 8th Latin American Theoretical Informatics Symposium*, LNCS 4957, pages 605–614, 2008. DOI: 10.1007/978-3-540-78773-0_52 39, 40

[70] E. Kranakis, D. Krizanc, and S. Rajsbaum. Mobile agent rendezvous. In *Proceedings of 13th International Colloquium on Structural Information and Communication Complexity*, pages 1–9, 2006. DOI: 10.1007/11780823_1 8

[71] E. Kranakis, D. Krizanc, N. Santoro, and C. Sawchuk. Mobile agent rendezvous search problem in the ring. In *Proceedings of International Conference on Distributed Computing Systems*, pages 592–599, 2003. DOI: 10.1109/ICDCS.2003.1203510 14, 15, 18, 20, 21, 31

[72] J. Lin, A. S. Morse, and B. D. O. Anderson. The multi-agent rendezvous problem. In *Proceedings of the 42nd IEEE Conference on Decision and Control*, volume 2, pages 1508–1513, 2003. DOI: 10.1137/040620552 91

[73] J. Lin, A. S. Morse, and B. D. O. Anderson. The Multi-Agent Rendezvous Problem. An Extended Summary. *Cooperative Control*, 309:451–454, 2004. DOI: 10.1007/b99788 91

[74] J. Lin, A. S. Morse, and B. D. O. Anderson. The Multi-Agent Rendezvous Problem. Part 2: The Asynchronous Case. *SIAM Journal on Control and Optimization*, 46(6):2120–2147, 2007. DOI: 10.1137/040620564 91

[75] N. Lynch. *Distributed Algorithms*. Morgan Kaufman, 1996. 5

[76] Y. Métivier, N. Saheb, and A. Zemmari. Randomized rendezvous. *Mathematics and Computer Science: Algorithms, trees, combinatorics and probabilities*, pages 183–194, 2000. 40

[77] Y. Métivier, N. Saheb, and A. Zemmari. Analysis of a randomized rendezvous algorithm. *Information and Computation*, 184(1):109–128, 2003. DOI: 10.1016/S0890-5401(03)00054-3 40

[78] D. Milojičić, D. Chauhan, and W. LaForge. *Mobility: Processes, Computers and Agents*. ACM Press, 1999. 8

[79] D. S. Milojičić, W. LaForge, and D. Chauhan. Mobile objects and agents (MOA). In *Proceedings of 4th conference on USENIX Conference on Object-Oriented Technologies and Systems-Volume 4*, pages 1–14, 1998. 1

[80] R. Motwani and P. Raghavan. *Randomized Algorithms*. Cambridge University Press, New York, 1995. 40

[81] George Pólya. Über eine aufgabe betreffend die irrfahrt im strassennetz. *Mathematische Annalen*, 84:149–160, 1921. DOI: 10.1007/BF01458701 40

[82] G. Prencipe. Corda: Distributed coordination of a set of autonomous mobile robots. In *Proceedings of European Research Seminar on Advances in Distributed Systems*, pages 185–190, 2001. 73

[83] G. Prencipe. On the feasibility of gathering by autonomous mobile robots. In *Proceedings of 12th International Colloquium on Structural Information and Communication Complexity*, LNCS 3499, pages 246–261, 2005. 55, 73

[84] D. G. Rajnarayan and D. Ghose. Multiple agent team theoretic decision-making for searching unknown environments. In *Proc. 42nd IEEE Conference on Decision and Control*, pages 2543–2548, 2003. DOI: 10.1109/CDC.2003.1273004 33

[85] N. Roy and G. Dudek. Collaborative robot exploration and rendezvous: Algorithms, performance bounds and observations. *Autonomous Robots*, 11:117–136, 2001. DOI: 10.1023/A:1011219024159 2, 8

[86] N. Santoro. *Design and analysis of distributed algorithms*. Wiley-Blackwell, 2006. DOI: 10.1002/0470072644 5

[87] F. Sarracco. *Mobile Agents Security: Algorithmic Approaches for Hostile Hosts Detection*. PhD thesis, Dipartimento Di Informatica E Sistemistica, Universita Di Roma 'La Sapienza', Italy, February 2006. 74

[88] C. Sawchuk. *Mobile Agent Rendezvous in the Ring*. PhD thesis, School of Computer Science, Carleton University, Ottawa, Canada, 2004. 14, 33, 37

[89] T. C. Schelling. *The Strategy of Conflict*. Harvard University Press, Cambridge, MA, 1960. 8

[90] W. Shi. *Using Mobile Agents For Black Hole Search With Tokens In Multi Networks*. PhD thesis, Carleton University, Ottawa, Ontario, Canada, May 2007. 74

[91] I. Suzuki and M. Yamashita. Distributed anonymous mobile robots: Formation of geometric patterns. *SIAM Journal on Computing*, 28(4):1347–1363, 1999. DOI: 10.1137/S009753979628292X 73

[92] D. L. Tennenhouse, J. M. Smith, W. D. Sincoskie, D. J. Wetherall, and G. J. Minden. A survey of active network research. *IEEE communications Magazine*, 35(1):80–86, 1997. DOI: 10.1109/35.568214 2

[93] L. Tesfatsion. Agent-based computational economics: Growing economies from the bottom up. *Artificial Life*, 8(1):55–82, 2002. DOI: 10.1162/106454602753694765 2

[94] G. Weiss. *Multiagent Systems: A Modern Approach to Distributed Artificial Intelligence*. MIT Press, 1999. 8

[95] M. Wooldridge. Intelligent agents. In G. Weiss, editor, *Multiagent Systems: A Modern Approach to Distributed Artificial Intelligence*, pages 27–77. The MIT Press, 1999. 1

Glossary

BHS	Black Hole Search problem, 67	
DM	Do not Move, 12	
DTA	Double Token Algorithm, 50	
GP	Gathering Problem, 75	
IC(*count*)	Increment variable *count*, 12	
IR-state	Imminent Rendezvous state, 51	
MA	Mobile Agent, 9	
MCC	Move one node Counterclockwise, 12	
MCL	Move one node Clockwise, 12	
PRAM	Parallel Random Access Memory, 3	
QMA	Query host for another MA, 12	
QT	Query host for Token, 12	
RAM	Random Access Memory, 3	
RD	Rendezvous with Detection, 17	
RP	Rendezvous Problem, 17	
RT	Release Token, 12	

Authors' Biographies

EVANGELOS KRANAKIS

Evangelos Kranakis received his B.Sc. (in Mathematics) from the University of Athens, Greece, in 1973 and his Ph.D. (in Mathematical Logic) from the University of Minnesota, USA, in 1980. He held academic positions at the Department of Mathematics of Purdue University, Mathematisches Institut of the University of Heidelberg, Germany, Computer Science Department of Yale University, USA, Universiteit van Amsterdam, and Centrum voor Wiskunde en Informatica (CWI) in Amsterdam, The Netherlands. He joined the School of Computer Science, Carleton University, Canada, in the Fall of 1991. He has published in the analysis of algorithms, bioinformatics, communication and data (ad hoc and wireless) networks, computational and combinatorial geometry, distributed computing, and network security. He became Carleton University Chancellor's Professor in 2006.

DANNY KRIZANC

Danny Krizanc received his B.Sc. from University of Toronto, Canada, in 1983 and his Ph.D. from Harvard University, USA, in 1988, both degrees in Computer Science. He held positions at the Centruum voor Wiskunde en Informatica, Amsterdam, The Netherlands, the University of Rochester, Rochester, New York and Carleton University in Ottawa, Canada before joining the Department of Mathematics and Computer Science at Wesleyan University in 1999. His research focus is the design and analysis of algorithms, especially as applied to distributed computing, networking and computational biology.

EURIPIDES MARKOU

Euripides Markou received his B.Sc. (in Physics) from the University of Ioannina, Greece, in 1993 and his Ph.D. (in Theoretical Computer Science) from the National Technical University of Athens, Greece, in 2003. He has been a postdoctoral research fellow at the Université du Québec en Outaouais, and at McMaster University, Canada, at the National and Kapodistrian University of Athens, Greece and at the Laboratoire Bordelais de Recherche en Informatique (LaBRI), France before joining the Department of Computer Science and Biomedical Informatics at the University of Central Greece in 2008. His research interests include the design of algorithms and the study of the computational complexity for problems especially in the areas of distributed computing, algorithmic game theory, computational geometry and bioinformatics.

Index